William Giles Atkins

History of the Town of Hawley, Franklin County, Massachusetts

From its First Settlement in 1771 to 1887, with family records and....

William Giles Atkins

History of the Town of Hawley, Franklin County, Massachusetts
From its First Settlement in 1771 to 1887, with family records and....

ISBN/EAN: 9783337099077

Printed in Europe, USA, Canada, Australia, Japan

Cover: Foto ©ninafisch / pixelio.de

More available books at **www.hansebooks.com**

HISTORY

OF THE

TOWN OF HAWLEY,

Franklin County, Massachusetts,

FROM ITS

FIRST SETTLEMENT IN 1771 TO 1887.

With Family Records and Biographical Sketches.

BY WILLIAM GILES ATKINS.

"Breathes there the man with soul so dead,
Who never to himself hath said,
  This is my own, my native land?
Whose heart hath ne'er within him burned,
As home his footsteps he has turned
  From wandering on a foreign strand?"

WEST CUMMINGTON, MASS:
PUBLISHED BY THE AUTHOR.
1887.

PREFACE.

In compliance with a long cherished desire to compile a work of this kind, the History of Hawley is herewith presented. The author does not present it with the expectation or desire of being noted as a historian, but to arrange in a substantial form the archives of his native town, adding such facts, reminiscences, statistics, incidents, sketches and general items, as shall interest the general reader, or at least those who have emanated from the old town, and their descendants.

We were aware from the first that the quality of the work would be in proportion to the amount of research made, and have endeavored to canvass thoroughly and carefully in its interests, still, there are omissions—the reader will supply them, there are errors—you will generously and kindly correct them.

In the arrangement of the work, the matter is unavoidably somewhat mixed, as material was constantly arriving after other matter of a kindred nature was in print. The family records, as furnished by the town records, are very incomplete, and in many cases disagree with records furnished by families themselves, but correctness has been the aim; others could have done better—if they would—but the lot fell on us.

In the compilation valuable assistance has been rendered, and special thanks are due to Town Clerk, Lucius Hunt and family, Rev. Henry Seymour, Mrs. Ann Eliza Scott and others of Hawley. Geo. D. Crittenden of Shelburne Falls, P. L. Page of Ann Arbor, Mich, P. F. Cooley of Pittsfield, Mrs Alfreda Stebbins of Deerfield, James M. Crafts of Whately, and others who have given acceptable aid. Copious notes have been taken from the records left by Mrs. Jerusha King, some of which date from the first settlement of the town, and are regarded in the main as authentic, also from Dr. Holland's "History of Western Massachusetts" and Evarts' "History of the Connecticut Valley."

There are also many to whom no thanks are due, who have not so much as answered our correspondence.

We now produce the result of these researches, hoping it will be acceptable to those of present and future generations. Let the reader follow the generations here recorded, associating with each the events of which they were the witnesses; follow them through their rough pioneering; through the dark days of war, and through their subsequent prosperity; note their joys and their trials, their hopes and their fears. By a little stretch of fancy place yourself among them and live over the quaint customs of the olden time, their manner of thought, of speech, of dress, of worship, of amusement, and it will not only make a reality of history but will introduce to you your ancestors as they really were.

It will be seen that an individual is but a link in the chain of humanity; that a lifetime, at the longest, is an hour on the dial, and that whatever we would that the past generations had done for us, it is our duty to do for those to come.

The following pages will portray the origin, rise and progress of one of the rural towns, peopled with a noble race, early inculcating the principles of virtue, temperance and religion. While we are forced to see its mild decay, we look with a degree of pardonable pride to those, past and present, who have been and now are wielding a power for good in the great drama of life. And while we regret the absence of so many from the ancestral acres and the paternal hearthstone, this fact must ever force itself upon us, that it is a good place in which to be born.

Finally, the history is dedicated to the sons and daughters of Hawley, wherever they are, in the hope that they may prove worthy of their ancestry in whatsoever things are true; in whatsoever things are honest; in whatsoever things are pure; in whatsoever things are lovely; in whatsoever things are of good report.

WM. G. ATKINS.

West Cummington, Mass., June, 1887.

CONGRATULATORY.

"I am rejoiced that its history is to be written."   P. L. PAGE.

"I wish you success in this, your good undertaking."
MRS. LOUISA M. HUNT.

"Success to you."   (REV.) HENRY SEYMOUR.

"Success in your worthy undertaking."   H. A. LONGLEY.

"I wish you success in your undertaking."   THOS. K. BAKER.

"Wishing you every success in your undertaking."
JAS. M. CRAFTS.

CONTENTS.

Outline History	Page 5
Hatfield Equivalent	6
Act of Incorporation	8
Organization	9
Local Titles	12
Cemeteries & Rev. J. Grout's Epitaph	13
Jonas King's Inscription	15
Schools and Highways	16
Ecclesiastictal History	17
Congregational Clergymen	21
Rebellion Record	23
Town Officers	26
Selectmen	28
Representatives and Directory	31
Town Farm	32
Mills and Manufactories	33
Stores and Hotels	35
Post Offices	36
Population and Early Settlement	37
First Thanksgiving and Young America's Military Record	38
Accidents, Fires, &c.	39
A Bear Story	41
Family Records	42
Marriages	69
Deaths	74
Miscellanies	83
In our Grandmother's days	88
The old Schoolhouse and Orthodoxy vs. Infidelity	91
Biographical Sketches	94
Bozrah	100
Natives Abroad	103
Personal Reminiscences of P. L. Page	109
Sketches and Incidents	111
Reminiscences of P. F. Cooley	117
Appendix	129
Index to Family Records	131

HISTORY.

OUTLINE HISTORY.

From the time of the first settlement within the limits of New England, at Plymouth, Mass., Dec. 1620, to the present time, the tide of emigration has been "Westward Ho." The arrival of the Mayflower having formed a nucleus, other emigration from Europe soon followed, and towns in the eastern part of the state were rapidly settled and organized. The first settlement in Western Massachusetts was made at Springfield, in May, 1636. In a few years other towns were founded up the Connecticut river, the Hadleys, Northampton, Deerfield, Northfield, Greenfield, &c. From this natural avenue civilization still pushed westward, particularly up the valley of the Westfield river, and up the Deerfield as far as Charlemont, leaving the entire territory of the Green Mountain range unknown to civilization for more than a century after the arable lands of the Connecticut valley had been opened as homes to the white man. As those desirable localities became filled up, the population, following the spirit of their ancestors, sought new fields of adventure, that they might enjoy civil liberty and religion according to the dictates of their own conscience, establish local government for themselves, appropriate the fertility of the virgin soil, which in those days

"Still on her bosom wore the enameled vest,
That bloomed and budded on her youthful breast."

Thus many people sought the primeval forest to rear homes, in pursuance of the spirit which has reigned ever since those days, that of going to the frontier, and beyond the border of civilization. So far as we know, the original settlers of all these mountain towns were from some portion of this state, all the way from the salt waters of Cape Cod to the Connecticut valley, and in some instances from towns west of the river. The pioneer settlers were generally from the old puritan stock, and, as a rule, adorned their religious profession, and early established churches and schools.

A large tract in the western part of the original County of Hampshire, now comprising ten towns, was sold at auction by the General Court, June 2, 1762. No. 7 of that series, afterward named Hawley, was bought by Moses Parsons for £875. Parsons in turn sold to other land-speculators; but those records are not attainable, and it is believed that none of the first proprietors became actual settlers. A portion of the east part of the town was known as the "Hatfield Equivalent," previous to the purchase of Parsons, which will be treated in a subsequent chapter. It is therefore reasonable to conclude that that portion was not included in the purchase of Parsons, it being previously owned by other parties.

The original town of Hawley was larger than at present; June 3, 1803, a tract was taken from the south side, and a strip from the north line of Cummington were united to form the town of Plainfield. The present town of Hawley contains about thirty square miles. It is bounded on the north by Charlemont, on the east by Buckland, on the south by Plainfield, in Hampshire County, and on the west by Savoy, in Berkshire County, making it the southwest corner town in Franklin County.

The natural features are broken and hilly, making a natural business center impracticable. Some of the south and east part of the town might be termed table-land, although the extreme eastern part has quite a descent towards Buckland, while the northeast portion descends in a like manner towards the Deerfield valley in Charlemont. Through the west part of the town a deep valley is traversed by Chickley's river, flowing north the entire length of the town into the Deerfield. Southeast of the center is the highest elevation in Franklin County, called "Parker's Hill." A similar elevation is also in the extreme south part of the town, called "Beals' Hill." On both of these peaks signal flags have recently been placed to assist in a U. S. topographical survey. The streams flow north and east, and help swell the waters of the Deerfield before reaching Shelburne Falls. The people have generally followed agriculture as an occupation, but water privileges have been utilized to some extent for manufacturing purposes, such as saw mills and other wood-working machinery and the tanning of leather with hemlock bark. But as the forests have become depleted and the population decreased, these latter industries are of less importance than formerly.

The point around which the most historic associations cluster is called the "square." This was for a long term of years the Mecca of the people of the town. Here was the first meeting house, where the people met alike for religious services and the transaction of town business. Here was also the first post-office, store and hotel, altogether making it the central business point. But in the lapse of time the business merged from that point and became scattered. In those primitive days the social and financial interests of towns were much more individualized and limited by geographical lines than at present.

Hawley is in latitude 42 1-2 degrees North, and about 73 degrees West longitude.

HATFIELD EQUIVALENT.

In 1659, in consideration of some services rendered, the General Court granted to Mr. Simon Broadstreet, afterward Gov. Broadstreet 500 acres of land, and also Maj. Daniel Denison 500 acres of land, with the privilege "that they might locate the same at any place west of the Connecticut River, provided that it be full six miles from the place intended for

Northampton meeting house, upon a straight line." Gov. Broadstreet had the first choice, and he chose Hatfield north meadows, beginning at the north end of the street and running north and west to the ponds. Maj. Denison took his north of the ponds, extending north on the river one mile, and west from the river 250 rods.

Immediately after this Hatfield was settled, and the inhabitants began to murmur about these grants. As they were not then set off from Hadley, that town induced Gov. Broadstreet to remove his claim and accept 1000 acres lying north of Major Denison's, and in addition they were to pay the Gov. £200. So after the transfer had been made they had a strip three miles long and 250 rods wide, taking all the meadow land for three miles on the river.

After Hatfield became a separate town she felt uneasy about this possession of so much of her best farm lands. So she petitioned to the "Great and General Court" for some redress for her grievance and the legislature, in 1744, gave them the lands lying adjacent to Huntstown, now Ashfield, in all 8064 acres as an equivalent for the lands originally granted to Broadstreet and Denison. The basis of the division of the Hatfield Equivalent was the valuation of estates for taxation, after the manner of the original division of the town of Hatfield in 1684. So people with large estates drew large lots, while those with small estates drew but a small proportion. "Verily to him that hath shall be given, and to him that hath not shall be taken away even that which he hath."

There were 83 recipients of this bounty, which included all the taxpayers of Hatfield at the time the grant was made, and parties who came into the town after the grant did not receive any of the land. The names of these 83 proprietors are given in the records, with the number of acres and rods given to each, together with the width of each lot, given in rods, feet and inches. The length of the lots is not given, but we conclude they were of uniform length, and that the width was established so as to give each one the amount of land required, and preserve this uniformity in length.

The proprietors of the grant met at Hatfield, on Monday, May 6 1765, and the following votes were passed relative to the Hatfield Equivalent.

Voted, that a way be laid out North and South through ye whole tract, half way from ye West way voted by ye town to ye West line of ye grant

Voted, two ways be laid from sd way to ye middle way in such places as ye Committee who shall stake out ye land shall judge best.

Voted, that two ways be laid by ye Committee as aforesaid from ye middle way to ye East way that runs through ye tract.

Voted, that a way be laid by sd Committee Two hundred rods North of ye Northermost way voted by ye Towne, which runs East & West and from ye East line till it meet with ye West line of ye grant.

Voted, that a way be laid in some convenient place by sd Committee from ye last mentioned way to run South Two hundred rods to ye way next South.

Voted, that each of ye ways agreed upon & voted at this meeting be four rods wide & so laid by ye Committee as not to divide any proprietor's lot.

Voted, by ye Proprietors, that they will draw division lots for their several portions in sd property, & that No. 1 begin at ye Southeast corner of ye tract, & ye lots be laid East & West as far as ye Northeast corner of Mr. Mayhew's farm. Then ye lots to be laid North & South, bounding North on ye Southway that runs East & West so to continue to ye East line of ye grant. Then to begin at East side of ye next range North & proceed to ye East way running through ye tract voted by ye town. Then to begin at ye North end of ye West range of ye first Division & to continue to ye South line. This completes ye first Division.

Voted, that No. 1 In ye second Division to begin at ye Northwest corner of ye tract & to run South throvgh the Westermost range. Then to begin at ye South end of ye adjoining range & to extend North to ye North line of ye grant, then to run East in ye South range of this Division & proceed to ye West side of ye grant. This completes ye second Division.

Voted, that when it so happens in each Division that a lot is not finished at ye end of a range it shall be completed at ye end of next range.

Voted, that the Proprietors will now proceed to stake & set out their land to each Proprietor his portion, & that Elisha Hubbard, David Wait, Elijah Morton, Lt. Bardwell & Ebenezer Cole be a Committee for that purpose.

Evarts, in the History of the Connecticut Valley, says that a portion of the Hatfield Equivalent was merged into the town of Plainfield, but whether the pioneer settlers bought of the original Hatfield proprietors, we are not informed.

ACT OF INCORPORATION.

Commonwealth of Massachusetts:

In the year of our Lord One thousand seven hundred and ninety-two. An Act to incorporate the Plantation of Number Seven, so called, in the County of Hampshire,* into a Town by the name of Hawley.

Be it enacted by the Senate and House of Representatives in General Court assembled, and by the authority of the same, that the aforesaid Plantation, bounded north on Charlemont, east, partly on Buckland and partly on Ashfield, south on Plainfield and west on the County of Berkshire, be and hereby is incorporated into a town by the name of Hawley, with all the powers, privileges and immunities that towns within this Commonwealth have or do enjoy.

*This was before the division of the original County of Hampshire.

And be it enacted by the authority aforesaid, that David Sexton Esq. be and hereby is empowered to issue his warrant, directed to some principal inhabitant of the town of Hawley, requiring him to notify the inhabitants of the said town, qualified as the law directs, to assemble and meet at some suitable place in said town and choose such officer or officers as towns by law are empowered to choose at their annual meetings in the month of March or April. In the House of Representatives February 1 1792. This bill having had three several readings passed to be enacted.

DAVID COBB, Speaker.

In Senate, February 6 1792.
This Bill having had two several readings passed to be enacted.

SAMUEL PHILLIPS, President.

Feb. 7 1792. By the Governor.

Approved, JOHN HANCOCK.

ORGANIZATION.

Now that the town had become incorporated and entitled to assume rank among the sister towns of the Commonwealth, the next duty incumbent upon the people was to form a municipal organization.

During the first years of the existence of the town the municipal and church interests were so closely identified that we give a condensed sketch of the records.

The warrant for the first town meeting was made by David Sexton, Esq. of Deerfield, issued to Edmund Longley, Esq., to notify the inhabitants of the town to meet at the house of Edmund Longley, on Monday, Apr. 2, 1792, to choose the necessary town officers.

The election resulted as follows; Town Clerk, Edmund Longley; Selectmen, Thomas King, Joseph Longley, Zebedee Wood, Amos Crittenden, and Ebenezer Hall; Treasurer, Joseph Longley; Constable, James Parker; Assessors, Zenas Bangs, Samuel Hitchcock, Zepheniah Lathrop; Tithingmen, David Parker, Whalen Hawkes, John Burroughs, Joseph Bangs, Thomas King; Sealer of leather, Zenas Bangs; Lumber nspectors, Nathan West, Elisha Wells; Highway Surveyors, Oliver Edgarton, George Eddy, Amos King, Ebenezer Burroughs, Arthur Hitchcock, Josiah Willard, David Parker, A. Rogers, John Taylor.

May 7, 1792, Voted to keep the 24th day of May as a day of fasting and prayer, and neighboring ministers were invited to participate.

Voted to raise £30 for schooling. Chose a committee of seven to divide the town into school districts.

Voted to raise £100 for the repair of highways. Voted to allow 4 shillings per day for work on highways until Sept. 1, and 3 shillings from that time, and the same for a good team.

Voted to raise £10 to defray town charges.

Voted to raise £20 for the support of the gospel, and to have preaching one half the time at Col. Longley's, and the other half at Abraham Parker's. Chose a committee of three to pitch a meeting house spot, and voted to abide their judgment.

Sept. 10, 1792, Voted not to accept the report of the meeting house committee, and chose another committee of seven for said purpose.

Sept. 27, 1792, Voted to choose a committee of three from out of town to fix a meeting house spot. Chose one from Dalton, one from Rowe and one from Conway.

Nov. 2, 1792, Voted to accept the report of the last committee.

Jan. 14, 1793, Voted to build a meeting house, 40 by 50 feet. Chose Joseph Longley, Thomas King, Edmund Longley, Nathan West and Hezekiah Wairiner to superintend the work.

Voted to apply to Mr Jonathan Grout to preach with us the ensuing season. An order was issued to several families, by order of the selectmen to the constable, to depart from the town. The reasons for issuing this order are not given. Other similar orders followed.

Oct. 25, 1793, Rev. Jonathan Grout ordained; council met at Edmund Longley's. Salary, £200, in semi-annual instalments. A remonstrance against setting off a part of the town to Plainfield was sent to the General Court.

July 7, 1794, Nathan West was chosen to provide a town stock of powder, leads and flints.

In 1795 the town appropriations were double the amount of those first made, in 1792.

The transactions of the town during the years 1795, 6 and 7 seem to be mainly directed to the location and building of a meeting house. Various committees were chosen from time to time for that purpose, and their action was invariably repulsed at the next meeting, and twelve reconsiderations of votes relative to proposed sites are recorded during those three years. The town records do not give date of buiding the house, but a record of March 5, 1798 says, voted to sell the pews in the meeting house; also April 2, voted to raise £50 to paint the meeting house. So from the import of those records it is reasonable to conclude that the house was built in 1797.

OTHER RECORDS.

May 6, 1799, Voted to accept a road from Camp rock west to Savoy line.

March 3, 1800, Voted to pay 25 cents a day for a man and the same for a team on the highways.

Nov. 15, 1802. Voted that the selectmen be a committee to remonstrate against a part of Hawley being set off to Plainfield.

Apr. 4, 1803. Voted that no cattle (except what is called yearlings) shall be allowed to run on the common the present year under the penalty of the law. Similar votes were passed during succeeding years.

Nov. 15, 1804, Voted, that a committee estimate the pew notes and say what each man shall pay on th dollar for paying Rev. Grout his salary. Dec. 26, 1805, Voted to send a representative to the General Court against the County being divided.

May, 1808, Voted to pay 25 cents a head for crows killed in town.

In 1808, the town sent a committee with a petition to the President to suspend the embargo.

Nov. 13, 1809, Voted to establish a school district on West Hill.

1810, Voted $ 300 for schooling.

1812, Voted that scholars shall be reckoned between 4 and 21 years of age. 1813, Raised $ 350 for schooling.

Nov. 7, 1814, Voted to choose a committee to enquire what proportion of provisions Mr. Grout's salary would buy now, compared to the worth when settled.

May 7, 1817, Voted to petition the General Court for assistance to build a bridge over the Deerfield river.

At the annual meeting. Mar. 6, 1818, the following rules for regulating town meetings were adopted. It would be well if business meetings at the present day could be governed by the same rules.

Meetings shall be opened within one hour after the time given in the notice, extraordinary cases excepted. When called at the opening of a meeting, we will take our seats and remain seated, except we rise to vote, speak, or leave the place of said meeting.

We will suspend all private business in time and place of said meeting. No person shall speak in meeting without leave of the moderator.

No person shall be interrupted by another except to call to order or correct a mistake. A person when speaking shall address the moderator.

No person shall speak more than once to one question until others who have not spoken shall speak if they desire it, nor more than twice without leave of the meeting.

The Moderator shall preserve decorum, speak to points of order, decide all questions of order, subject to an appeal to the meeting, on motion regularly seconded.

We will aid the Moderator in the discharge of his duties, who is bound to keep the person having leave to speak to the point in question or call him to order.

The Moderator shall not delay business by introducing any subject in the time of a meeting that is not regularly before the meeting by a warrant.

Dec. 6, 1821, Voted to take measures to procure a stove for the meeting house, and chose a committee for that purpose. Previous to that time there had been no arrangements for warming the house. Some of the women carried foot-stoves, a square frame about eight inches square into which were placed some hot coals from the fire-place, on which they would set their feet for warming, and during the intermission on Sunday they would go to the nearest house and replenish the coals. Think of people going four or five miles to church in winter, and sometimes on horseback at that, going into a house where the semblance of fire had never been, and remaining through two long services. It would be a question at the present day, whether the necessities of church services would compensate for such self-imposed barbarous treatment!

In 1821, Voted to deposit the military stores in the meeting house.

Nov. 12, 1838, Voted to employ only such teachers as can teach writing. From this it may be inferred that the art of writing was not a necessary qualification for teachers in the public schools previous to that time. April 22, 1839, Chose a committee of ten to consider the evils of perpetuating slavery, and report at a future meeting.

In 1840, 115 militia men were enrolled; in 1853, 132.

April 3, 1848, Voted to build a town house near the center of the town. Chose Freeman Atkins, Clark Sears and Harmon Barnes as a committee for that purpose. Appropriated $500 for schools.

Apr. 7, 1851, Voted to buy a farm for the support of the poor. Chose Levi Holden, Calvin Cooley and Charles Baker as committee for that purpose. Appropriations in 1867. Schools, $900, Highways, $1200, Town charges, $1000. The same appropriations were made in 1886.

Mar. 23, 1870, Voted to pay 25 cents per hour on highways. The change in prices of labor during seventy years may be noticed by reference to a vote passed in 1800, when 25 cents a day was paid on highways.

LOCAL TITLES.

Several localities in town by common consent have received local titles, a brief account of which we give.

"Bozrah," north part of town, adjoining Charlemont, includes one school district. Received its name from the fact that some of the first settlers came from Bozrah, Ct.

The site of the first business interests of the town, including church, stores, post-office and hotel, was termed the "Square," or "Common." It was a sightly elevation of several acres, a little east of the territorial center of the town.

In the primitive days, probably before 1780, Mrs. Baker, wife of Timothy, was matched against another woman, to see which would make the largest hasty pudding. Mrs. Baker made hers in a five pail kettle, and came out triumphantly the "pudding head" of Hawley. That circumstance gave the title "Pudding Hollow" to that neighborhood, embracing school district No. 1, lying in north part of the town.

"Potash Hill" was the name formerly given to a very steep highway leading from Pudding Hollow to the Square. The name was given from the circumstance of a potash manufactory being formerly located near the road.

"Forge Hollow," later called West Hawley, received its name from being the site of a forge where iron was made in the early part of the present century, the ore being received from "Forge Hill," on the old road leading from West Hawley to Pudding Hollow. The same water privilege has been continuously used, and is now owned and occupied by Willis Vincent.

"King Corner," southwest corner of town. In the spring of 1772, Thomas King came from Brimfield and bought 1000 acres of land for one dollar an acre. His descendants of the fourth and fifth generation still remain in the neighborhood, and until the death of Warriner King in 1877, the original name of King had continously lived there, covering a period of 105 years.

"Hallockville," on the Plainfield line, with an extensive water power, was occupied in 1826 by Leavitt Hallock, who done a large business for about twenty years in tanning and sawing lumber.

"Fullerville" received its name by Clark W. Fuller having established a mercantile and manufacturing business, about 1855.

"West Hill" is a neighborhood in the west part of the town, being divided from King Corner by the upper waters of Chickley's river, flowing from Savoy.

CEMETERIES.

The first burial place in town was near the territorial center, nearly a mile southeast from the present town house, on what is known as the Childs lot. Although not in close proximity to any settlement then made, it was established there with the supposition that there would be the central business point of the town. The spot is away from any road, and is known to but few. It was proposed a few years ago to mark the spot by setting a stone at each corner of the place occupied. About twenty were buried there. Before the first meeting house was built a cemetery was opened about a mile east of its site. This is virtually called the oldest one in town. Here are buried representatives of many of the oldest families, those who organized and manipulated the early transactions of the town, including Parson Grout, who was pastor for almost half of the church history of the town. His epitaph is as follows:—— "This stone was erected by the first parish of Hawley to the memory of the Rev. Jonathan Grout, who departed this life June 6, 1835, in the 73d year of his age, and the 42d of his ministry. He was the first minister in Hawley. Great unanimity among his people prevailed during the ministry of this devoted servant of Christ."

Among the inscriptions there are the names of Longley, Warriner, Smith, Mantor, Crosby, Newton, Holden, Doane, King, Hitchcock, Sanford, Vining, Field and Hall. The oldest inscription found there is that of Nathaniel Parker, died Mar. 25, 1789.

When the old meeting house was removed and a new one built, about a mile and a half south, in 1847, a new cemetery was opened a little south of the present church. This was largely due to the efforts of Calvin S. Longley. Some of the names found there are Scott, Clark, Wood, Williams, Bassett, Longley, Eldridge and Harmon.

Before the advent of the present century a burying ground was opened at Pudding Hollow, where their families have been buried. This cemetery is second in size as well as age, and contains the names of Baker, Hall, Crowell, Sears, Crosby, Atkins, Rice, Bangs and Taylor.

Sometime about 1820, a cemetery was started in the old sixth school district, a little east of the Graves place, so called. Here are buried the King and Rice families who early settled in the old 7th district, Col. Noah Joy and wife, and families bearing the names of Marsh, Sprague, Hunt, Holden and Griggs. Here is the largest headstone in town, over the remains of Jonas King, a representation of which is given on the opposite page. The slab stands six feet above the ground, is nearly three feet in width, 2 1-2 inches thick, the top being two inches convex.

At West Hawley, a cemetery was founded as early as the church there perhaps earlier, where many of the people of that part of the town have been buried. It is on a kind of plateau as seen from the road, and its approach is quite steep and difficult. Here are found the names of Vincent, Stiles, Curtis, Sears, Turner, Ford, Atkins, Brackett, Fuller. (See Sketches and Incidents.)

There is also a private family burying ground on the farm of Phineas Starks, in the southwest part of the town, where about a dozen have been buried.

Like others, these burial places are the receptacles of many high hopes and aspirations, and where the "willows of grief bend deepest." The grounds are usually well kept, and the most of them are annually mowed.

"As the long train
Of ages glides away, the sons of men,
The youth in life's green spring, and he who goes
In the full strength of years, matron and maid,
The bowed with age, the infant, in the smiles
And beauty of its innocent age cut off,-
Shall, one by one, be gathered to thy side,
By those, who, in their turn, shall follow them."
Bryant.

Sacred
to the memory of

Mr. JONAS KING,

the venerable Father
of the distinguished

Rev. JONAS KING, D. D.

Missionary to Palestine & Greece.

On being asked by a Friend if he felt any regret in parting with his Son, as a Missionary to the Heathen, this Father in Israel replied, "God so loved the world that he gave his only begotten Son, that whosoever believeth in him should not perish but have everlasting life."
And should I withhold my only Son from obeying the command of our ascended Saviour, "Go ye into all the world and preach the gospel to every creature. Mr. KING was one of the first settlers in Hawley.
He lived, in example & precept, a life of holiness.

He died
September 20th 1832,
Aged 78 years.

Having a blissful faith in Jesus Christ and an unshaken hope of a glorious immortality. His last words were:
"How often must my pulses beat,
Before my joys shall be complete?"
Come Lord Jesus! come quickly.

Ask you my name, 'Tis JONAS KING,
Beneath these clods I lie,
In life I suffer'd much by sin,
And sin caused me to die!
But by the blessed Jesus, I
Do hope to rise again,
I then shall live and never die,
And praise the Lord.   Amen.

Fac-simile of an inscription in the cemetery in the old sixth school district in Hawley.

SCHOOLS.

The people have always taken an active interest in their common schools, and have appropriated liberally for their means. That interest seems to be cotemporary with the church interest. The long list of professional and influential men, past and present, emanating from the town attests the quality and efficiency of her school work.

In 1792, the year of the organization, £30 was voted for schooling. Three later the amount was doubled, and in 1797, £75 was raised, in 1840, $500, and at the present time the appropriation is $900, showing a uniform increase, with the onward march of progress.

May 7, 1792, a committee, consisting of Edmund Longley, Ebenezer Hall, Abel Parker, Amos Crittenden, Zebedee Wood, Abel Warner and Jonathan Fuller, was chosen to divide the town into school districts.

May 6, 1793, £210 was voted to build seven schoolhouses, £30 to each, and the following persons were appointed as building committee:

District No. 1, Reuben Cooley, Zenas Bangs, Ebenezer Hall; No. 2, Joseph Lathrop, Ichabod Hawkes; No. 3, Elijah Hammond, Asa Blood, Asher Russell; No. 4, Hezekiah Warriner, Samuel Hitchcock, David Parker; No. 5, Arthur Hitchcock, Phineas Scott; No. 6, Ebenezer Borland, John Campbell; No. 7, Thomas King, Simeon Crittenden. It was voted that the several school-houses be built fit to keep a winter school in by the first of November next.

In later years there has been eleven districts, one of which was called the "Union," being a union with Plainfield. That house being burned some years ago, that district was disbanded. When the legislature made the school district system optional with towns, Hawley with many other towns abolished her school districts, in 1867. Soon after, some of of the territoral lines were changed, condensing some of the districts, so that at present there are eight districts which support six months of schooling in each year.

For some time about ten years ago, the matter of supervision was given to ladies, Mrs Bethiah S. Barton, and Miss Sarah Eastman, each successfully manipulating the business at different times, but usually it is managed by a committee of three members. The average wages paid to teachers is about $4.50 per week.

HIGHWAYS

were early deemed a necessity, and it is evident that roads were in operation before the incorporation of the town, as a vote passed that spring appropriated £100 to repair highwaws. The appropriations for roads and bridges have uniformly been in excess of those made for any other matter. The first settlers located their roads over the rugged hills, tradition saying that they considered the hills less incumbered by muddy roads than the valleys, also that they wanted to be in a position to see the smoke from each others' houses. But as the valleys became more settled and the surrounding towns made through travel more of a necessity, more feasible routes were utilized.

The transactions of the town furnish copious records relative to highways, many transcripts having been made during its entire history, and many old roads have been discontinued, and superseded by new ones.

The old "Potash Hill" road was originally the main avenue from Pudding Hollow, West Hill, and Forge Hollow, for all their church-going, town and mercantile business; now that steepest of all highways is discontinued, and a new road from the town house to the Theophilus Crosby place. Formerly the road from Forge Hollow to Pudding Hollow was over Forge Hill, but for many years, a road down the valley of Chickley's river, although a greater distance, has been a more feasible route. A portion of the road from the town farm to Savoy line, has recently been discontinued, and one built of a much easier grade.

Many similar changes have from time to time been made, as changes in business interests demanded. In some cases these changes have left once prosperous homesteads isolated from travel, and many have been deserted in consequence. In 1795, £200 were appropriated for roads, and now for a score of years the appropriation has been $1200.

The highway districts, have highway surveyors, chosen annually, having charge of their respective localities, the tax-payers usually "working out" their tax, the price allowed per hour being stipulated by the selectmen. The road on the banks of Chickley's river has often suffered by destructive floods. Oct. 4, 1869, all the bridges on the stream were carried away, also several wash-outs.

May 6, 1799, the town voted to accept a road from Camp rock to Savoy line. This started near the Theophilus Crosby place, and probably is an old road running by the Graves place, the Thomas King, afterward the Ezra King place, the John Hadlock place the Elijah Marsh place, the Warriner King place, now the town farm, the Jonathan Fuller place to the Daniel Rice place, on the Savoy line. This road was about three miles in length, and a portion of the middle of its route has long been discontinued.

ECCLESIASTICAL HISTORY.

The organization of the church antedates the incorporation of the town thirteen years. Sept. 16, 1788, an ecclesiastical council met at the house of Samuel Hitchcock, and the ministers on the organizing council were Revs. Nehemiah Porter and Jacob Sherwin of Ashfield, John Emerson of Conway, and Jonathan Leavitt of Charlemont. The number constituting the church was twenty, ten males and ten females, and were as follows: —Thomas King, Nathaniel Rudd, Daniel Burt, Silas Hitchcock, Samuel Hitchcock, Abel Parker, Daniel Parker, Benjamin Smith, Nathaniel Parker, Josiah Graves, Mary Burt, Mary Hitchcock, Phebe Parker, Sarah Parker, Thankful Hitchcock, Martha Parker, Rebecca Parker, Abigail Graves, Sarah Cooley and Elizabeth Smith.

The articles of faith and the covenant then adopted, were the same that the church has retained until the present time.

From 1781 to 1793 the records are lost, and excluding those twelve years, 55 more members were added previous to 1800. In 1807, 33 were added, in 1816, 118, in 1822, 18, in 1825, 44, in 1828, 14, in 1831, 64, in 1832, 31. In 1834 the membership was 205, which was the highest number ever attained. Its present membership is about sixty.

For about fifteen years after the organization of the church it was without a settled pastor. Rev. Jacob Sherwin of Ashfield preached for it a part of the time, the meetings being held in dwelling houses and barns. The first pastor was Rev. Jonathan Grout, who was ordained and installed Oct. 23, 1793. The sermon on the occasion was preached by Rev. Dr. Lyman of Hatfield, with whom Mr. Grout studied theology. He was born in Westboro, in 1763, and graduated at Harvard college in 1790. He was the pastor of the church until his death, nearly forty-two years, having passed all his ministerial life in town. A neighboring clergyman, probably Dr. Shepard of Ashfield, thus wrote concerning him. "Mr. Grout was a diligent, laborious, and successful minister. He loved his people, and his people loved him. He was truly a practical man. His sermons were not highly wrought, but contained important truth, adapted to the circumstances of his people.

He was emphatically sociable, hospitable, kind-hearted and the impression which he left behind him was good, that his people generally appreciate the ministry and respect the minister." (For his epitaph see "Cemeteries.")

During the last year of Mr. Grout's ministry, he was so infirm as to be unable to perform the duties of his office, and May 14, 1834, Rev. Tyler Thatcher was installed as his colleague. Mr. Thatcher was born in Princeton, Sept. 11, 1801, and graduated at Brown university in 1824. Before his settlement here, he preached in several places. His ministry here was about nine years. He afterwards went to California, where he spent the remainder of his life in preaching and teaching. He had a strong, logical mind, and was a great reasoner. Among his hearers was Hezekiah Warriner, who was somewhat skeptical, and many were the discussions they had on points wherein they differed, and many were the sermons in which Mr. Warriner was specially had in mind.

Still he paid liberally for the minister, at which some expressed surprise, but he said it was no more than fair, for he had more than his share of the preaching. Mr. Thatcher died in California, Dec. 4, 1869.

After the dismissal of Mr. Thatcher, in 1843, the pulpit was supplied by Rev. John Eastman four years, and Rev. Wm. A. Hawley two years. The third pastor, Rev. Henry Seymour, was installed Oct 3, 1849. He was born in Hadley, Oct. 20, 1816, graduated at Amherst college in 1838, studied theology at the Union seminary in New York city, and his first settlement was in Deerfield, Mar. 1, 1843, where he remained about six years. After a ministry of seventeen years in Hawley, he was dismissed, and the pulpit was supplied by Rev. R. D. Miller about three years. In June, 1870, Mr. Seymour was again invited to supply the pulpit, which he engaged to do with the understanding that he was to preach but one sermon each Sabbath, his health being infirm, which he has continued to do until the present time.

Until the year 1825, there was but one meeting house and one church in town, and the people came from all parts of the town to the old sanctuary on the hill. It was at no little inconvenience that many of them gathered there, and it is a strong testimony in favor of the people that they came so constantly from such distances, over such roads, and in such weather, and before the church was warmed with stoves as now. The result was that the old church was usually well filled with devout worshippers.

As the population of the west part of the town increased, it was thought best to organize a church and build a house there, which was done in 1825. Forty-four members, 19 males and 25 females, were dismissed from the parent church, and organized a church at West Hawley. The church was suppled for fifteen years by Rev. Urbane Hitchcock, Dr. Packard, and his son Theophilus and others.

The first settled pastor was Rev. Moses Miller, who was installed over it May 20, 1840. Mr. Miller was born in Worcester, Nov. 23, 1776, graduated in 1800. His first settlement was at Heath, where he remained 35 years. The second pastor was Rev. John Eastman. He was born in Amherst, July 16, 1803. He was not a college graduate but received the degree of A. M. at Amherst College, and studied theology with Dr. Packard of Shelburne, and after having preached in various places in the state of New York, he was installed at West Hawley. Nov. 11, 1847. After remaining with the church about eight years, he was dismissed, and the pulpit was supplied at brief intervals by Revs. Lewis Bridgman, Joseph B. Baldwin, Robert Connell and Robert Samuel. Mr. Eastman was again recalled, and preached as long as he was able from age and infirmity. Mr. Eastman was one of the old school Calvinistic ministers and was quite an impressive preacher. Jan. 5, 1851, he delivered a sermon at the funeral of Rufus Sears, which was published in pamphlet form at the request of his parishioners. Mr. Eastman has two daughters at Wellesly, Mass., who are eminent teachers, Julia A., who is a writer and author, and Sarah who was at one time superintendent of schools in Hawley.

In the interval between Mr. Eastman's two pastorates, Rev. Jeremiah Pomeroy preached there several years. His oldest son, William M., entered Amherst college from Hawley, and after graduation, took up journalism, and has been successively editor of the Springfield Republican, Springfield Union, Pittsfield Eagle, and at present is editor of the Orange Journal.

Since Mr. Eastman's second pastorate the pulpit has been supplied by Rev. Lincoln Harlow, Rev. Mr. Guild, and at present by Rev. F. J. Grimes, all of Charlemont, conducting one service each Sabbath. Present number of members, forty-five.

The first Sabbath school in town was organized the first Sabbath in June, 1820, with twelve teachers. It has been continued ever since, and at present is superintended by Enos Harmon, with a membership of 89, and 9 teachers. The West Hawley church also maintains a Sunday-school, and at the time of Mr. Samuel's pastorate, it is said that the entire congregation were regular attendants, with the exception of two men who could not be induced to attend.

The present meeting house on the hill was built in 1847; the first one at West Hawley was built in 1825, and the present one in 1847.

Thomas King and Joseph Bangs were among the early deacons of the town. At West Hawley the deacons have been Rufus Sears, Ebenezer Hall, Zenas Bangs, Ebenezer Crosby, Millo T. Carter, Samuel Hall, Frederick H Sears and Samuel Williams.

The singing in both of these churches has been performed by old fashioned choirs, which were strengthened by occasional singing schools, and in the "palmy days" the singing was quite powerful and impressive. Edwin Scott and Willis Vincent are at present the choir leaders.

These churches are of the Congregational denomination, and are the only churches that have ever been formally organized in town, but the Methodists and Adventists have held services to considerable extent at different times.

To show the stern discipline and the prevailing sentiment in regard to church government half a century ago, we copy from the records of a church meeting held Jan. 28, 1835:— "Church met at the meeting house. Dea. Lathrop presented a complaint against Bro. Theodore Field for absenting himself from the public worship and ordinances of God. Voted that a communication be addressed to Bro. Field in behalf of the church." We predict that if the same discipline relative to church attendance was enforced now, the list of complaints would be very copious.

THE CONGREGATIONAL CLERGYMEN

from the town have been as follows:—

Rev. Urbane Hitchcock was born in Hawley in 1782; graduated at Williams in 1806, and was ordained to the ministry at Dover, Vt., in 1808. He was one of the early ministers at West Hawley.

Rev. Jonas King, D. D., was born in Hawley, July 29, 1792; read the Bible through before he was six years old, and every year thereafter; graduated at Williams in 1816; studied theology at Andover; was ordained as evangelist in 1819; went as a missionary with Pliny Fisk to Jerusalem in 1823, and in 1828 became a missionary to Greece, where his labors in behalf of the struggling Greeks attracted much attention, and resulted in promoting the welfare of the oppressed inhabitants. His last visit to America was in 1865.

Rev. Pindar Field was born in Sunderland, May 1, 1794, but removed to Hawley the following year, studied at Williams, but graduated at Amherst in 1822, and was licensed Dec. 1824.

Rev. Isaac Oakes was born in Hadley, June 10, 1795, graduated at Williams in 1820, and was ordained at Salem in 1823.

Rev. Thomas H. Wood was born in Bozrah, Ct., in 1772, but removed with his parents to Hawley in 1775, graduated at Williams in 1799, and was licensed to preach in 1803. He died in 1846.

Rev. Marshall L. Farnsworth was born in Hawley in 1799, graduated at Union in 1825, and was licensed soon after. He died at Danby, N. Y., in 1838.

Rev. Oliver A. Taylor was born at Yarmouth, Aug. 18, 1801, but came to Hawley when two years old. His parents were poor and unable to educate their children, but gave them the example of devout, consistent lives, and encouraged them in their efforts to educate themselves, with what success is shown by the four ministers the family produced. At the age of twenty, Oliver started to walk five hundred miles to enter Alleghany College, Pa., but graduated at Union in 1825, studied at Andover, completing in 1829, and was licensed in April of that year. He became very learned, and died in 1821.

Rev. Timothy A. Taylor was born in Hawley, Sept. 7, 1809, graduated at Amherst in 1835, and at Andover in 1838.

Rev. Rufus Taylor was born in Hawley, March 24, 1811, graduated at Amherst in 1837, and at Princeton in 1840.

Rev. Jeremiah Taylor, the fourth brother of this noted family, was born in Hawley, June 11, 1817, graduated at Amherst in 1843, and at Princeton in 1847.

Rev. Alvah C. Page was born in Hawley, March 17, 1806, and was ordained as an evangelist at Charlemont in 1831.

Rev. Thomas A. Hall was born in Hawley, Sept. 2, 1813, graduated at Williams in 1838, and was licensed in 1840.

Rev. O. W. Cooley was born in Hawley, June 18, 1816; graduated at Williams in 1841, and was licensed in 1845.

Rev. Foster Lilley was born in Hawley, June 6, 1812; graduated at Williams in 1838, and was licensed in 1840.

Rev. Alfred Longley was born in Hawley, Nov. 10, 1809; studied at Oberlin, and was licensed in 1843. He died March 16, 1851.

Rev. Moses M. Longley was born in Hawley, June 14, 1815, studied at Amherst, and graduated at Oberlin in 1845. He was ordained an evangelist in 1846.

Rev. Elijah Harmon was born in Hawley, March 22, 1835, graduated at Amherst in 1861, graduated at the Hartford Theological Seminary in 1867, ordained at Winchester, N. H. Oct. 17, 1867, installed at Wilmington, Mass., Dec. 15, 1885.

Rev. Joseph G. Longley was born in Hawley May 24, 1823. He became a Congregational minister, but died before he had engaged in pastoral labors.

As Methodist ministers Hawley has furnished Judah Crosby, Silas Leonard and Proctor Marsh. Three natives of the town have served acceptably as Advent ministers, viz: Rufus Starks, born March 21, 1812, Clark R. Griggs, born March 6, 1824, and Dennis Sears. The last six were not graduates, but were licensed.

NOTE. The title D. D. should have been affixed to the names of Rufus and Jeremiah Taylor. The four Taylors were brothers, sons of Jeremiah Taylor. Their mother was a woman of more than ordinary strength of mind and of eminent piety. She died at the house of her son-in-law, Dea. Freeman Hamlin, in Plainfield, Oct. 22, 1857 aged 80 years.

The three Longleys were brothers, sons of Gen. Thomas Longley.

The following ladies have married ministers or professional men:— Mary, daughter of Gen. Thomas Longley, married Rev. Stephen R. Riggs, L. L. D., for many years a missionary to the Dakota Indians. She is the Mary of that interesting book by Dr. Riggs, "Mary and I."

Nancy Newton became the second wife of her pastor, Rev. Tyler Thatcher. Angeline, daughter of Otis Longley married Dr. Ashley, a western clergyman. A daughter of Theophilus Crosby married a minister. Mary Bassett was one of the early graduates of Mount Holyoke Seminary, and was for a number of years a prominent teacher in Ohio. She is now the wife of Benjamin M. Ludden, M. D., of East Lynn, Ill. The widow of Dr. Forbes, an early physician, married Dr. Moses Smith, who remained in town as a practitioner about thirty years.

Olive, daughter of Capt. Edmund Longley, married Hezekiah Ryland Warriner, L. L. D., a brilliant teacher in Greenfield and Deerfield, afterward a law student in the office of Henry T. Grout, L. L. D., in Philadelphia, and died soon after being admitted to the bar, in the midst of a rising reputation.

REBELLION RECORD.

Hawley bore a creditable part in the War of the Rebellion. She was represented in all the regiments that went from Western Massachusetts, to the front, and at the last enrollment more than half of the able bodied men liable to do military duty were already in the field. Many were the loyal sons who went forth to battle for the old flag in the hour of its peril, some to give their lives in the service for which they fought, and fill soldiers' graves on traitors' soil, some to be brought home and buried by loving hands, beneath their native skies, and still others to return, wearing their laurels. Not only did the people respond to the country's necessities as soldiers, but contributed liberally in appropriations for state aid, bounties, clothing and other articles of comfort.

Nov. 5, 1861, the town voted to abate all the town taxes assessed upon volunteers belonging to the town who have entered the service.

Aug. 29, 1862, Appropriated $300 for state aid to soldiers' families.

Oct. 15, 1862, Voted to pay a bounty of $100 to each volunteer enlisting under the last calls of the president, and credited to the quota of the town.

Mar. 2, 1863, Appropriated $500 for state aid to families of volunteers.

Nov. 3, 1863, Appropriated $1059 78 for volunteers.

Mar. 7, 1864, Voted to raise $1000 for state aid to soldiers' families.

Apr. 25, 1863, Voted to raise a sufficient sum to fill all quotas up to the present time, not to exceed $125 to each man. A similar vote was passed June 27 of that year.

Amount of money raised and paid by the town and private subscriptions, exclusive of state aid, $17,175. Amount raised and paid by the town and afterwards refunded by the state, 2,842 63.

The ladies of Hawley contributed $525 in clothing and other articles of comfort for the soldiers, which were forwarded by them to the front.

The following is a list of those who served in the war as soldiers:—

J. William Doane, enlisted Sept. 4, 1862, in Co. E, 52d Regt. He was promoted to corporal at Camp Miller, Greenfield, was discharged in Aug. 1863, returned to civil life, lives on the farm adjoining his birthplace.

Geo. C. Brayman, enlisted Sept. 4, 1862, in Co. E, 52d Regt. He was wounded in the leg June 14, 1863, had the leg amputated, and died in the hospital at Baton Rouge, La, July 3, 1863.

Henry C. Damon, enlisted Sept. 4, 1862, in Co. E, 52d Regt., discharged in Aug., 1863, now a farmer, in Meriden, Ct.

Homer F. Damon, enlisted Sept. 4, 1862, in Co. E, 52d Regt., discharged in Aug., 1863, now a tinner in New Britain, Ct.

Edwin Warriner, enlisted Sept. 4, 1862, in Co. E, 52d Regt., discharged in Aug. 1863, and died June 15, 1882, of consumption.

David C. Clark, enl. Sept. 4, 1862, Co. E, 52d Regt., dis. Aug. 1863.

Lucius Hunt, enlisted Sept. 4, 1862, in Co. E, 52d Regt. He was sick in hospital, and was discharged July 17, 1863, by reason of disability. His brother Josiah went to Louisiana after him and brought him home. He lives at his birthplace in Hawley.

Nathan B. Baker, enlisted Sept. 4, 1862, in Co. E, 52d Regt. Discharged in Aug. 1863, and is a farmer in Savoy.

Theodore Marsh, enlisted Sept. 4, 1862, in Co. E, 52d Regt. was discharged in Aug. 1863 and lives in Whitingham, Vt.

Noah Baker, enlisted Sept. 4, 1862, in Co. E, 52d Regt. He was shot through the right side at the battle of Port Hudson, La., June 14, 1863, died instantly, and was buried where he fell.

Edwin Baker, enlisted Sept. 4, 1862, in Co. E, 52d Regt. He was discharged in Aug. 1863, and is a druggist at Shelburne Falls.

Thomas A. Hall, enlisted Sept. 4, 1862, in Co. E, 52d Regt. He died at Baton Rouge, La., Jan. 20, 1863. of typhoid fever.

Elijah Harmon, enlisted Sept. 4, 1862, in Co. E, 52d Regt. discharged Aug. 1863, and is now a clergyman in Wilmington, Mass.

Thaxter Scott, enlisted Sept. 4, 1862, In Co. E, 52d Regt., was discharged Aug. 1863, and is a farmer in Hawley.

Clinton H. Dodge, enlisted Sept. 4, 1862, in Co. E, 52d Regt. was discharged Aug. 1863, and is a farmer in Hawley.

Otis B. Wood, enlisted June 14, 1861, in Co. H, 10th Regt., promoted to Corporal Apr. 11, 1863, and Sergeant, May 1, lives Turners Falls.

Newell S. Rice, enlisted May 3, 1861, in Co. E, 10th Regt. He followed the fortunes of his regiment till 1863, when he re-enlisted, receiving the veterans' bounty and served through the war. He lives in Ohio.

John H. Larabee, enlisted May 28, 1861, in Co. B, 10th Regt. Served his term of enlistment, and now lives at the west.

Edwin P. Cobb, enlisted Oct. 1, 1861, in Co. C, 27th Regt. discharged July 19, 1865, and lives in Hawley.

Alfred L Mantor, enl. Oct. 1, 1861, in Co. C. 27th Regt. Killed in battle May 6, 1864, at Petersburg, Va.

Francis W. Mantor, enl. Oct. 1, 1861, Co. C, 27th Regt. Died of diphtheria Oct. 3, 1862, at Washington, N. C.

Luther Eddy, enl. Oct. 1, 1861, Co. C. 27th Regt.

Samuel Woffenden, enl. Oct. 1, 1861, Co. C. 27th Regt.

Edmund Longley, enl. Oct. 1, 1861, Co. C. 27th Regt. Died of consumption, at New York, Sept. 7, 1863.

John A. Grout, enlisted July 2d 1862, in Co. C, 27th Regt., was discharged July 19, 1865, and lives in California.

Charles H. White, enlisted July 2, 1862, In Co. C, 27th Regt.

William J. Sanford, enlisted Nov. 13, 1861, in Co. C, 31st Regt., now lives at Hartford, Ct.

Robert H. Eldridge, enl. Nov. 21, 1861, Co. B. 31st Regt. Taken prisoner at Brashaer city, July 3, 1863, and died July 6.

Albert Clark, enlisted April 30, 1861, Co. H, 10th Regt. Lives in Hawley.

Clark F. Sprague, enlisted Nov. 22, 1861, in Co. B, 31st Regt. Discharged June 18, 1862, on account of ill health, and died March 25, 1863 of consumption, at his fathers' house in Hawley.

Asher B. Sprague, enlisted Nov. 22, 1861, in Co. B, 31st Regt., and lives in Hawley.

Henry C. Mason, enlisted Nov. 13, 1861, in Co. B, 31st Regt. He was wounded in the thigh at Port Hudson plain, July 3, 1863, died in the hospital July 17, of chronic diarrhea.

Albert E. Marsh, enlisted Nov. 22, 1861, in Co. B, 21st Regt. Resides in Northampton.

Chandler Hathaway, enlisted Oct. 15, 1861, in Co. C, 31st Regt. Died at Baton Rouge, La., Mar. 12, '63, of congestive chills and buried there.

Erastus S. Kinney, enlisted July 24, 1862, in Co. F, 34th Regt., now lives in Ashfield, and receives a pension of $30 a month.

Chandler H. Blanchard, enlisted July 24, 1862, in Co. F, 34th Regt. He was wounded in battle in the leg and carried to the rear by a comrade, who had also been wounded. He lives in Adams and carries a wooden leg.

Peter L. Baker, enlisted July 24, 1864, Co. F. 34th Regt. He was severely wounded in the thigh, but served out his term of enlistment. He was a splendid marksman and stated that during his term of service he probably discharged his rifle 2000 times and never without taking careful and deliberate aim. He died at Bernardston Vt. Jan. 8, 1879 of consumption.

Alonzo Helm, enlisted July 24, 1862, Co. F. 34th Regt.

Samuel M. Hall, enlisted July 24, 1862, Co. F. 34th Regt. He was shot through the neck and instantly killed in battle.

Everett W. Blanchard, enlisted Oct. 1863, Co. F. 34th Regt. While insane he was killed by jumping from a third story window in Annapolis, Md.

Freeman L. Cobb, enlisted Aug. 14, 1862, Co. H. 37th Regt. Promoted as Corporal.

Sidney P. Wood, enlisted Aug. 14, 1862, Co. H. 37th Regt. Wounded in the shoulder at the battle of the Wilderness, May 5, 1864. died in May at Fredericksburg.

Edward Peck, enlisted Aug. 14, 1862, Co. H. 37th Regt. He was discharged Mar. 17, 1863, at camp near White Oak church by reason of disability caused by not properly recovering from measles. He returned home, and died of consumption, Jan. 27, 1865.

Edmund H. Sears, enlisted Aug. 14, 1862, Co. H. 37th Regt. Accidentally shot by a comrade near Spottsylvania Court House May 11, 1864, on picket duty was brought home and buried in Hawley.

Ira Larkins, enlisted Aug. 14, 1862, in Co. H. 37th Regt. Appointed Corporal Aug. 15, 1862, appointed sergeant March 1863, killed in battle May 18, 1864, carrying the colors.

Albert Vincent enlisted Aug. 14, 1862, Co. H. 37th Regt. Appointed orderly sergeant Sept. 1, 1862. Wounded May 1863, commissioned 1st Lieutenant July 31, 1864. Commissioned Captain March, 1865.

Freeman Brackett, enlisted Aug. 14, 1862, Co. H. 37th Regt. Appointed Corporal Mar. 20, 1863. Died of typhoid fever at City Point July 10, 1864, brought home and buried in W. Hawley.

Alonzo F. Turner, enlisted Aug. 14, 1862, Co. H. 37th Regt. Wounded July 3, 1863, transferred to V. R. C. Lives in Hawley.

William A. Hallock, enlisted Aug. 14, 1862, Co. K. 23rd Regt.

John Brown, enlisted Sept. 2, 1864, Co. C. 17th Regt. He served only 8 months to the close of the war, saw no fighting or hard service, and received about $1100 as bounty, state aid and wages. Removed to Kansas.

TOWN OFFICERS. 1792—1886.

The following have served as Town Officers since the organization of the town, including the Moderators of the Annual March meetings:—

Date.	Moderator.	Town Clerk.	Constable.
1792	David Sexton	Edmund Longley	James Parker
1793	Joseph Longley	"	David Parker
1794	Thomas King	"	"
1795	Hezekiah Warriner	"	Joseph Longley
1796	Elijah Field	"	Zenas Bangs
1797	Joseph Longley	"	Obed Smith
1798	Zephaniah Lathrop	"	Zimri Longley
1799	Hezekiah Warriner	"	David Parker
1800	"	"	William Sanford
1801	Joseph Bangs	"	Thomas Longley
1802	Zephaniah Lathrop	"	Argalur Pixley
1803	Hezekiah Warriner	"	Oliver Carr
1804	Joseph Bangs	"	Edmund Longley, Jr.
1805	"	Ebenezer Hall	"
1806	Edmund Longley	"	Abel Dinsmore
1807	Joseph Buttrick	Thomas Longley	John King
1808	Zephaniah Lathrop	"	"
1809	"	"	"
1810	"	"	Simeon Crittenden

Date.	Moderator.	Town Clerk.	Constable.
1811	Zephaniah Lathrop	Thomas Longley	Elias Goodspeed
1812	Edmund Longley	"	Abel Dinsmore
1813	Zephaniah Lathrop	"	Ebenezer Hall
1814	Zenas Bangs	"	John King
1815	Zephaniah Lathrop	"	Elias Goodspeed
1816	"	"	"
1817	"	"	Eben Crosby
1818	Zenas Bangs	"	Abel Parker
1819	"	"	John Hall
1820	"	"	"
1821	"	"	"
1822	Zephaniah Lathrop	"	Theophilus Crosby
1823	"	"	"
1824	Noah Joy	"	
1825	"	"	Hezekiah Warriner Jr
1826	"	"	Ebenezer Crosby
1827	John Tobey	"	John Hall
1828	Noah Joy	"	Cushing Shaw
1829	"	Moses Smith	"
1830	Thomas Longley	,,	"
1831	Noah Joy	Thomas Longley	Quartus Taylor
1832	"	"	Abel Longley
1833	John Vincent	"	Bardine Damon
1834	Noah Joy	"	Calvin Longley
1835	"	"	Ezra Brackett
1836	"	"	Eben Crosby
1837	Thomas Longley	Moses Smith	"
1838	John Tobey	"	"
1839	"	"	Calvin Longley
1840	Noah Joy	"	Freeman Longley
1841	John Vincent	Edmund Longley Jr	Harmon Barnes
1842	John Tobey	Anson Dyer	Bardine Damon
1843	William F Longley	Calvin S Longley	William O Bassett
1844	"	"	Harmon Barnes
1845	John King	"	Ezra King
1846	No record	"	Elijah Longley
1847	Clark Sears	John Vincent	"
1848	"	Calvin S Longley	Samuel Hall
1849	"	George Lathrop	"
1850	"	"	J V King
1851	John Vincent	Calvin S Longley	Elijah Longley
1852	"	"	Jonathan Vincent

Date·	Moderator.	Town Clerk.	Constable.
1853	Wm O Bassett	Calvin S Longley	Harmon Barnes
1854	Clark Sears	"	Atherton Hunt
1855	Wm O Bassett	"	"
1856	"	"	"
1857	"	"	B Parsons Mansfield
1858	Clark Sears	"	Atherton Hunt
1859	"	Dennis W Baker	A G Ayres
1860	F H Sears	"	"
1861	"	"	"
1862	Wm O Bassett	"	"
1863	John Vincent	"	"
1864	Clark Sears	"	J W Doane
1865	John Vincent	"	E F Longley
1866	Clark Sears	"	Samuel A Clark
1867	Wm O Bassett	F H Sears	"
1868	"	"	"
1869	Clark Sears	Freeman Atkins	J W Doane
1870	John Brown	"	James Doane
1871	W E Mansfield	Harvey Baker	H W Starks
1872	Wm O Bassett	Edwin Scott	"
1873	"	"	E P Hunt
1874	W E Mansfield	"	"
1875	Wm O Bassett	J W Doane	Ambrose K Sears
1876	F H Sears	"	Joseph A Hitchcock
1877	Frank Simpson	"	"
1878	"	"	"
1879	F H Sears	"	Edwin Scott
1880	W E Mansfield	Lucius Hunt	"
1881	J W Doane	"	"
1882	"	"	A K Sears
1883	"	"	Joseph A Hitchcock
1884	"	"	Lewis Hall
1885	Frank Simpson	"	Adna Bissell
1886	Charles Crittenden	"	Joseph A Hitchcock

SELECTMEN

The following have been the selectmen of the town from 1793 to 1886.

1793	Joseph Longley	Thomas King	Nathan West
1794	"	"	Ebenezer Hall
1795	Hezekiah Warriner	Zephaniah Lathrop	"
1796-7	"	Moses Clark	"
1798-9	"	Zephaniah Lathrop	"
1800	"	Moses Clark	"
1801	"	Zephaniah Lathrop	"
1802	Edmund Longley	Sylvanus Smith	"
1803	"	Hezekiah Warriner	"
1804	"	Sylvanus Smith	Joseph Bangs
1805	Nathaniel Newton	Hezekiah Warriner	Joseph Bangs
1806-7	"	"	Joseph Buttrick
1808	Edmund Longley	"	"
1809	"	"	Zenas Bangs
1810	Nathaniel Newton	"	"
1811	Zephaniah Lathrop	"	"
1812	Joseph Buttrick	Hezekiah Warriner	"
1813	"	Zephaniah Lathrop	"
1814	Hezekiah Warriner	Ebenezer Hall	"
1815	Zephaniah Lathrop	Joseph Buttrick	Noah Joy
1816	Hezekiah Warriner	Zenas Bangs	"
1817	Edmund Longley Jr	"	"
1818	"	" William Bassett	"
1819-20-21	Zenas Bangs	"	"
1822	Edmund Longley Jr	"	Hezekiah Warriner
1823	" "	"	John Tobey
1824-25	"	" Noah Joy	"
1826	Wm Sanford	"	"
1827-28	Edmund Longley Jr	Noah Joy	"
1829	John Vincent	"	"
1830	Thomas Longley	"	Warriner King
1831	Edmund Longley Jr	Calvin Cooley	John Vincent
1832	Warriner King	John Tobey	"
1833	"	Calvin Cooley	"
1834	John Tobey	Samuel Hall	Joshua Vincent
1835	Jonas Jones	Calvin Cooley	"
1836	Edmund Longley Jr	Clark Sears	"
1837	Thomas Longley	Warriner King	John Vincent
1838	Calvin Cooley	George Lathrop	"
1839	"	"	Samuel Hall

1840 Calvin Cooley	John Vincent	Wm F Longley
1841 Thomas Longley	Warriner King	Francis Mantor
1842 John Tobey	Clark Sears	Samuel Hall
1843 Levi Harmon	"	George Lathrop
1844 "	"	Calvin Cooley
1845 John Vincent	George Lathrop	Freeman Atkins
1846 Clark Sears	"	Freeman Longley
1847 Samuel Williams	"	"
1848 Clark Sears	Levi Harmon	Wm O Bassett
1849 John Vincent	Freeman Atkins	Nelson Joy
1850 Clark Sears	"	Samuel Clark
1851 "	Otis Longley	Milo T Carter
1852 Wm O Bassett	Harvey Baker	Joshua W Tobey
1853 "	Nathan Vincent	"
1854 "	Joshua W Tobey	Harvey Baker
1855 "	"	J G Longley
1856 "	"	Harvey Baker
1857 "	John Vincent	Charles Baker
1858 S A Clark	"	B P Mansfield
1859 Calvin Cooley	"	David Vincent
1860 Charles Baker	"	A G Ayres
1861 Wm O Bassett	Charles Crittenden	Elijah Field
1862 "	"	F H Sears
1863 Clark Sears	A G Ayres	Willis Vincent
1864 Charles Baker	Edwin Scott	A G Ayres
1865 "	"	Elijah Field
1866 Clark Sears	W E Mansfield	Willis Vincent
1867 Wm O Bassett	"	Harvey Baker
1868 "	E S Carter	"
1869 "	John Vincent	E P Hunt
1870 "	John Vincent	E S Carter
1871 W E Mansfield	F H Sears	Willis Vincent
1872 "	E S Carter	Harmon Barnes
1873 Charles Crittenden	"	C H Dodge
1874 "	M H Vincent	"
1875-6 Wm O Bassett	Lewis J Hall	Walter Sears
1877 "	"	Isaac C Vincent
1878 Charles Crittenden	"	C H Dodge
1879-80 "	Elijah Scott	Willis Vincent
1881 "	Willis Vincent	J A Hitchcock
1882 "	C H Dodge	E S Carter
1883 "	"	Lewis J Hall
1884 "	Lewis J Hall	J W Doane
1885-6 J W Doane	C H Dodge	Foster R King

REPRESENTATIVES TO GENERAL COURT.

1794, 1795, 1796, 1797, 1798, 1800, 1802, 1803, 1804, 1805, 1806, 1807, 1809, Edmund Longley; 1810, 1811, Zenas Bangs; 1812, 1813, 1814, 1816, Thomas Longley; 1818, Ebenezer Hall; 1824, Thomas Longley; 1826, Edmund Longley Jr.; 1829, Moses Smith; 1832, John Tobey; 1833, Edmund Longley Jr.; 1836, Calvin Cooley; 1837, 1838, John Vincent; 1839, 1840, Calvin Cooley; 1841, 1843, George Lathrop; 1844, Clark Sears; 1847, Thomas Longley; 1849, Nelson Joy; 1850, George Lathrop; 1851, Clark Sears; 1853, Nathan Vincent; 1860, John Vincent; 1864, Rev. Henry Seymour; 1868, Clark Sears; 1879, Clinton H. Dodge.

Nov. 3, 1794, Theodore Sedgwick was chosen Representative to Congress from the Western District.

DIRECTORY.

The occupation of those engaged exclusively in agriculture will be understood; those engaged wholly or in part in other occupations will be noted.

Francis W. Atkins, Asahel R. Atkins, Albert B. Atkins, Roswell Baker, Wm. H. Brackett, Wm. O. Bassett, Justice of the Peace, Harmon Barnes, Joseph Buskitt, laborer, Adnah Bissell, produce dealer, Francis Barnard, Edna J. Barnard, Noel Barber, Charles Clemons, Nathan Clark, Nathan Clark Jr., Henry Clark, Herbert L. Clark, School Committee, Warren Clark, David Clark, Samuel A. Clark, Tyler T. Clark, Edwin P. Cobb, laborer, Charles Crittenden, lumber dealer, Herbert L. Crowell, Stillman Carter, Martin V. Cressy, Elias Carrier laborer, Porter J. Carrier, laborer, Joseph H. Carrier, S. Russell Chaflin, carpenter, Mattoon Church, Charles Davis, J. Wm. Doane, Selectman, Clinton H. Dodge, Selectman, Newell Dyer, Thomas E. Eldridge, sawmill proprietor, Ira Fuller, Wm. A. Fuller, Albert Gould, mechanic, Lemuel Gould, George Gould, Gilbert Gould, Wilson Gould, Clarence Gould, Dennis Gibbons, wood chopper, A. C. Galbraith, Levi Hawkes, William Hawkes, Joseph A. Hitchcock, Constable, Elijah B. Howes, Frank J. Howes, Clarence Hubbard, laborer, Lewis J. Hall, lumber dealer, Wm. F. Harris, Enos Harmon, Charles Harmon, Frank Hillman, Henry A. Holden, J. N. Hamilton, Francis Holden, Asa Holden, Erastus Graves Frank A. Holden, Atherton Hunt, Lucius Hunt, Town Clerk, Elisha Hunt, Chester F. Hunt, Chester L. Hunt, Charles Hunt, Myron C. Harwood, Mc Kendree Hicks, Lewis Hicks, wood turner, Henry A. Hicks, employee of Davis Mining Co., J. U. Houston, blacksmith, Fred N. Haskins, laborer, Frank Ingraham, teamster, Lauriston King, butcher, Alfred King, teamster, John F. King, laborer, Foster R.

King. merchant, selectman. Charles Kinney, William Kenny, A. J. Kendall, carpenter, School Committee, Lewis Longley, laborer, Daniel Larkins, laborer, Nathan Mason, W. E. Mansfield, Pension Agent, Justice of the Peace, Albert S. Maynard, Allen Murdock, James. M. Parker, Alvin H. Parker, Sylvester Rice, George W. Rice, Rufus Rice, Matthew D. Rice, John Rashford, Oscar Rood, Seth Sears, Royal Sears, Roswell Sears, Edwin W. Sears, F. H. Sears, Charles Sears, George W. Sears, Ambrose K. Sears, Postmaster, Ebenezer Sears, Albert F. Sears, School Committee, James F. Sears, Walter Sears, Dennis Sears, Sylvester Sears, John Sprague, Asher B. Sprague, Chauncey Stafford, George H. Stetson, M. Sprague, Manly Stetson, Erwin Scott, Walter Scott, Elijah H. Scott, saw mill proprietor, Edwin Scott, Postmaster, Phineas Scott, Willard F. Scott, Henry Seymour, Clergyman, Bartholomew Scanlan, Michael Scanlan, George K. Starks, grist mill and saw mill proprietor, Phineas Starks, Morris D. Starks, Henry W. Starks, blacksmith, Rowland Stiles, Elijah Shaw, Jr. Frank M. Simpson, Geo. H. Taylor, Henry Taylor, Dennis A. Taylor, Alonzo F. Turner, saw mill and wood working shop, Nathan Tyler, Henry Tyler, William Thayer, William R. Thayer, Lewis W. Temple, Warriner K. Vining, hoop manufacturer, Willis Vincent, Justice of the Peace, saw mill, and rake manufacturer, Mark H. Vincent, rake manufacturer, Isaac C. Vincent, Samuel Williams, Wm. L. Warfield, Justin B. Warriner, Henry B. White, Melvin White, laborer, Justin B. Wood, William Wait, Waldo T. Ward, Benjamin C. Wilbur, David White.

TOWN FARM.

At a town meeting, April 7, 1851, it was voted to buy a farm for the support of the poor. Previous to that time the keeping of the town poor had usually been done by boarding them with the lowest bidder, or by the Overseers of the poor, which were the selectmen, making a contract with parties to keep them. They were not all kept at one place, but went where circumstances dictated.

The committee chosen to buy a farm was Levi Holden, Calvin Cooley and Charles Baker, and they purchased of Dea. Samuel Hall the place known as the Warriner King farm, in the southwest part of the town.

It was urged by some as a reason for buying an alms-house, that some who had in part been maintained by the town and allowed to remain with their friends would prefer to support themselves and escape the odium of going to the "poor-house," as all who received aid from the town were required to go there. The selectmen annually hire a man and his wife as overseers of the farm and house, who receive a stipulated salary, averaging about $250, who are required to keep an exact account of receipts and expenditures. The first of April is the time adopted for making a change of overseers, and dairying is the chief source of revenue

The following, and their wives have been the overseers of the town farm. 1851-2 Leouard Joy; 1853-4 S. S. Hemenway; 1855 to 62 Proctor Marsh; 1862-3 Henry Barton; 1863 to 1870 Phineas Starks; 1870 John Brown; 1871 to 73 Henry Barton; 1875 Horace Todd; 1876 to 1879 Daniel Larkins; 1879 to 84 Phineas Starks; 1884 Levi Hawkes; 1885 Geo. Turner; 1886 Charles Davis.

At the annual town meeting, March, 7, 1853, a code of rules was adopted regulating the house and its inmates, which reflects upon the civilization of the 19th century. It received the title "Black Laws," copies of which were placed upon the records, and posted in the house.

It was the subject of a poem written and published at the time by Miss Mary Taylor entitled "Northern Oppression."

MILLS AND MANUFACTORIES.

It is evident that the erection of mills, particularly sawmills and gristmills, engaged the attention of the earliest inhabitants. The oldest record found is furnished by Mr. Geo. D. Crittenden of Shelburne Falls, made by his great grandfather, Zebebee Wood, at a meeting of the inhabitants of No. 7, held Feb. 24 1778, at the house of Samuel Hitchcock, Thomas King, moderator. The record reads, "Voted Thomas King to go and talk with the proprietors, and see what they will do about building mills and getting on the rest of the settlers."

Sometime about 1790, Capt. Simeon Crittenden started in the extreme south part of the present limits of the town, and operated a sawmill and grist mill. He afterwards sold to Joel Rice, who came from Conway, paying 2000 silver dollars for the property. He conveyed it to his sons, Luther and Daniel, who operated it until 1826, when it was bought by Leavitt Hallock, who built a large tannery in 1827, also built other sawmills, and established a large and flourishing business which continued until the tannery was burned, Feb. 11, 1846. It was rebuilt in 1848, but never was operated as a tannery. A sawmill was afterward operated in the building by Homan Hallock, and other wooden ware has been manufactured there, but that interest is now extinct. Half a mile down the stream, Alonzo F. Turner built a sawmill and shop for various manufacturing, about twenty years ago, which is still operated.

A little further down, Warriner King and Jonathan Fuller built a saw mill in the early part of the century, which was afterward burned.

Mr. King rebuilt, also added a shop, in which he made broom handles. These have been operated by A. G. Ayres, Wm. A. Turner, A. F. Turner, and Geo. K. Starks who now occupies the mill, the shop having been abandoned and taken down. Just below this point, Horace and David Thayer built a turning shop about forty years ago, which is now occupied by Geo. K. Starks as a grist mill. At Fullerville, a sawmill and other wood-working machinery has for a long time been occupied by successive parties. Half a mile from this point up the Savoy branch, John Miller built a mill about 1850, and afterward sold to Edward Peck, who added machinery for making butter boxes and various kinds of handles. The disastrous flood which visited all the Northern states, Oct. 4, 1869, swept away the dam and buildings, leaving only bare rocks where once was heard the busy hum of industry.

At West Hawley, a water privilege was utilized at the beginning of the century for the manufacture of iron, the ore being obtained from a mine near by. Elias Goodspeed was one of the operators. The buildings were burned and the forge abandoned. They were rebuilt, and have been used for various kinds of manufacturing. Willis Vincent has occupied and owned the place for the last thirty years, for making broomhandles, rakes, &c., and for a time run a grist mill in connection with the other business. Austin Pease built a tannery about 1835, which was operated by himself, and afterward by Howes & Sears, and was abandoned in 1855. Chester Upton once operated a shop for making handles near the residence of William Wait. Jonathan Brackett built a sawmill about forty years ago, just below Isaac C. Vincent's, afterward owned by Clark Sears, now abandoned. About 1836, John and Phineas Starks built a sawmill on Fuller brook which they run for a term of years. It was destroyed by a freshet, and never rebuilt.

Chickley's river, flowing through the west part of the town, furnishes the best water powers, although others have been successfully used. Before 1790, Moses Rogers had a grist mill near the present town house. Here Mr. Rogers was killed in 1808, while cutting ice from the water wheel. This privilege has long been utilized for a sawmill and turning shop, and has been owned by D. W. Baker, Harrison Colby Lewis J. Hall and others. The first mill proprietor in the east part of the town is believed to be a Mr. White. Dea. Levi Eldridge early built a sawmill now run by his sons. Joshua Vincent and Healy Newton once owned a mill towards the Buckland line. On the Bozrah brook small powers have been employed to operate clothing works and shops, and Charles Crittenden has for some time owned a sawmill there. An abandoned mill-site was once improved by Abraham Parker near the old meeting house. Soon after 1800, Elisha Hunt and Zenas Thayer built a sawmill where Theophilus Crosby formerly lived, a little east of where Chester F. Hunt now lives. After being used a few years it was burned one fall about Thanksgiving time. The neighbors turned out, drew and hewed timber, employed John Hadlock as carpenter, and put up another mill during the winter, and had it running the next spring. This was used for a term of years and then abandoned.

Many years ago a small tannery was built near where Atherton Hunt lives, which was operated by horse power and hand power.

The trades have been represented in proportion to the wants of the people of a rural community. John Hadlock was for a long time one of the carpenters of the town, and many buildings are now standing which he built. Lewis Cobb was also an old time carpenter. Russell S. Chaffin has recently located at West Hawley as a carpenter, and built a house which he occupies. Chester F. Griggs was one of the town shoemakers, and used to go around with his "kit" of tools and make up the annual stock of boots and shoes for each family. Warriner King and Phineas Starks each done quite a local business at making and mending for their neighbors. Mr. King used to say that he frequently earned enough on his bench in an evening to pay a hired man a days' wages. Zebedee Wood, who came from Connecticut to Hawley in 1784, was a tanner and shoemaker before coming there, and continued the business to some extent after coming. A blacksmith was one of the fixtures at the "Square" when that was the business of the town. J. U. Houston is now the blacksmith in the vicinity of the church, and Henry W. Starks at Fullerville. In the palmy days of Hallockville, Horace Elmer was the blacksmith there, Ira Angell the shoemaker and T. E. Eaton the tailor. Mr. Elmer afterwads done blacksmithing at West Hawley.

Charles Crittenden and Lewis J. Hall of this town are doing a large business at lumbering in Monroe, under the firm name of Crittenden and Hall. They have a steam mill which they have recently moved from Savoy, where they also done an extensive business. Several shops in town turn out chair stock which is sold to manufacturers in Worcester County.

STORES AND HOTELS.

Zebebee Wood is believed to have kept a small stock of goods before 1790 at his house, and Joseph Hubbard is said to have opened the first regular store. This stand was soon after occupied by Joshua, Wm. F. and Calvin S. Longley in the order named. William Sanford opened an opposition store near by, and Gen. Thomas Longley kept a store there at one time, which is now one of the only two buildings left standing on the "Square." Whitney Hitchcock and Jonas Jones began merchandising about 1833, and were succeeded by Lucius L. Clark and Leonard Campbell. Calvin S. Longley kept a store near the present church until his death, which is now kept by his son-in-law, Edwin Scott. At West Hawley, stores have been kept by James Mantor, Harvey Baker, T. S. Allen, A. G. Ayres, C. W. Fuller, Foster King and Manly Stetson, the two last still in business. About 1850, a union store was started at West Hawley, being No. 497 of the New England protective Union, which prospered for several years, one year the dividend paid to the stockholders being 42 per cent, but by some disastrous turn in the tide of affairs the stock became below par and the business closed.

At Hallockville, Leavitt Hallock conducted a store during the time of his business operations there.

Joshua Longley and Wm. Sanford kept opposition hotels near the first church while that was the center of business. Noah Joy built and opened a hotel at South Hawley in 1830, which he kept until his death in 1843. He was succeeded by Levi Holden, and Henry Clark, who kept it until 1865 when it was burned. Clark Fuller done a small business in that line in connection with his other business at Fullerville.

POST OFFICES.

Three Postoffices have been established in town, with the following Postmasters. The date of appointment of the first Postmaster in each place is the date of the establishment of the Office.

HAWLEY.

Postmaster.	Date of App't.	Postmaster.	Date of App't.
Joshua Longley,	Dec. 29, 1817	Eliza Longley,	Apr. 22, 1858
William F. Longley,	Mar. 3, 1838	Edwin Scott,	Sept. 25, 1862
Calvin S. Longley,	July 1, 1841		

SOUTH HAWLEY.

Noah Joy,	May 26, 1832	Matthew E. Hyde,	May 27, 1857
Nelson Joy,	June 29, 1853	Henry Clark,	Apr. 9, 1860
Levi Holden Jr.	Mar. 31, 1854		Discontinued Jan. 15, 1866

WEST HAWLEY.

Theodore S. Allen,	Oct. 7, 1850	Aaron G. Ayres,	July 2, 1867
Henry Howes,	May 13, 1852	Mark H. Vincent,	May 22, 1868
Edson B. Legate,	Apr. 27, 1854	Willis Vincent	Apr. 11, 1878
Stephen K. Hitchcock,	Sept. 11, ,54	Ambrose K. Sears,	Jan. 17, 1882
Willis Vincent,	Apr 29, 1857.		

The Postoffice at Hawley has been continuously conducted by the same family, representing three generations, since its establishment, covering a period of nearly seventy years, Edwin Scott, the present incumbent, being a member of the family by marriage.

The first mail was a weekly mail to and from Northampton, giving mail facilities to several intervening towns. Later, a tri-weekly mail has been run through, between Plainfield and Shelburne Falls. Among the carriers were Wm. J. Shattuck, Wm. M. Cleveland and J. F. Gurney. At present, a daily mail connects with the railroad at Charlemont, carried by H. S. Packard. The first mails at West Hawley were received semi-weekly from Charlemont, the people sometimes "taking turns" in carrying it, the receipts not paying expenses to the Department. Now a tri-weekly mail through from Charlemont to Adams. It is a common practice for carriers to receive and distribute mail matter to families on their route, for which a stipulated sum is annually paid by the parties.

POPULATION.

1772	22	1850	881
1776 Collonial,	244	1855	774
1790	539	1860	671
1800	878	1865	687
1810	1031	1870	672
1820	1089	1875	588
1830	1037	1880	592
1840	977	1885	545

The following figures are from the Assessors' books for 1886:—
    Value of Personal property, $31,648
    Value of Real Estate, $119,626
    Total, $151,274

No. of Horses, 147, Cows, 336, Sheep, 470, Neat Stock, 280, Swine, 124, Houses, 119, Acres, 17969,

The following were the products of the town in 1880.

Farms, 107, Hay, 2173 tons, Butter, 46997 lbs, Eggs, 12101 doz, Potatoes, 66 acres, 5505 bushels, Corn, 111 acres, 4116 bushels, total value of products, $42,911. Capital invested in lumbering $3500, value of product $2000.

EARLY SETTLEMENT.

Mrs. Jerusha King has furnished what is believed to be the most authentic account of the settlement of the town. Her grandfather, Thomas King, gave her the account in her early years, which she placed on record

In the spring of 1771, Noah Strickland settled where Edwin Warriner formerly lived, Fariel Burt and Samuel Hitchcock settled just east of the old cemetery, Adonijah Taylor located down the hill toward Pudding Hollow. In 1772, Thomas King came from Brimfield and located where his son Ezra has lived, Timothy Baker settled where Martin V. Cressy lives, and Reuben Cooley bought where Elijah Howes lives, making seven families who came during the first two years of the town's settlement. (Other families following will be noted in the family records, as far as known.) In the fall of 1772, occured the

FIRST THANKSGIVING.

During the summer, thes seven families fully realized the hardships and privations of a pioneer life, and felt a strong desire to return to their old homes and enjoy Thanksgiving with their friends; but as travelling in those days was only on horseback or with ox teams it was hardly possible for them to go. Mr. King proposed that they have a Thanksgiving and have all the town meet at one place. Accordingly, each family made preparations, and all met at Mr. Burt's. Their number was 22, which included every person in town. Their supper consisted of baked meat, puddings, chicken pie, mince pie made of bear's meat, apple pie made of apples brought from Conway, bread, &c. When their meal was nearly ready, one of the women remarked that they had everything necessary but milk to put in their tea. Mr. Taylor said, "Give me a pail and I will go and milk my horse." He had driven his farrow cow, harnessed to a sled to convey himself and wife. He also drew his wood and did other work, with the same team. When supper was ready, they all stood around the table, when God's blessing was invoked upon the food, they took seats and partook of the meal with thankful hearts, also thankful for the pleasant interview they had enjoyed. After supper, Mr. King read a portion of Scripture and read a hymn from the Psalter (the most approved hymn book in those days;) then offered prayer.

Soon came the parting and dispersing to their homes, which closed the first Thanksgiving in Hawley in 1772. In those seven families there were but 3 professors of religion, Mr. King and wife and Timothy Baker.

YOUNG AMERICA'S MILITARY RECORD.

A history of Hawley would be incomplete without giving a little military episode which happened nearly 40 years ago. About 1847, a party of boys in their teens, organized themselves into a company of infantry, the project being originated and mainly executed through the influence of Clark W. Fuller, one of the oldest of their number. These amateur soldiers were uniformed with red stripes on the legs of their pants, red belts, wooden swords and plumes of domestic manufacture, the officers having a uniform to distinguish their rank. Edwin A. Atkins was the first captain, and wore a handsome plume, a relic of the Plainfield company of state militia which had but recently been disbanded. The first parade was at Hallockville, with 18 men in rank and file. As time progressed, the interest and members increased, and one Fourth of July the company went to Savoy to assist in observing "the day we celebrate." Soon a small cannon mounted on wheels was brought into use, the exercises assuming the role of a company of artillery. On one occasion the company divided, receiving some help from outside parties, and arranged themselves for a sham fight, one party taking the woods, the other an open field adjoining. After several attacks and repulses, the party in the woods succeeded in capturing the cannon from the other side and won the field. The ambitions of the company soon required a larger gun. A second hand cannon was found, weighing 180 pounds, which was bought by subscription, each member contributing according to his means. At this time the headquarters of stores and ammunition was at Fullerville, and by sundry transfers of shares, quite a per cent of the stock was owned in West Hawley, (meaning the near vicinity of the church, postoffice, &c.,) and a kind of rivalry and hostility arose between these two factions. The West Hawley boys claimed a control of the cannon a part of the time, and one night they clandestinely took it and carried it to their own domain. By this time the contest was hot and the feeling bitter, the defeated party using all kinds of stratagem to recapture it. On one occasion the West Hawley boys became the aggressors by going to a point near Fullerville, discharging the cannon, and quickly retiring with it, a part of them remaining, apparently guarding the treasure. This had the desired effect in calling out a party of their antagonists which succeeded in gobbling up a wooden stick which had been brought as a feint, and the deception was complete. This of course, increased the feud between the two neighborhoods until the older people sympathized in the matter. Suffice it to say the cannon was never returned, and afterward disappeared, tradition saying that it was sunk in an old ore bed on "Forge Hill." After the usual changes caused by the lapse of time the matter was in a measure forgotten. The military company described in the first of this sketch was not formally disbanded, but seemed to die a natural death. A new cannon has for several years been owned in that part of the town which is called into requisition on holidays, its ownership not being influenced by the history of its predecessors.

ACCIDENTS, FIRES, &C.

The following records have been collected from various sources, and it is a matter of regret that so many are without date. Many years ago, Thomas Pixley was killed by a falling tree when at work on the farm now owned by Wm. O. Bassett. Moses Rogers was killed in the winter of 1808, while cutting ice from the water wheel in his mill, near the present town house. He went out to the mill one morning before breakfast, and not returning, search was made, and he was found crushed between the wheel and the wall. It was supposed that the wheel started sooner than he expected, and drew him in.

Sylvester Sears was drowned just below the bridge near Lewis W. Temple's, Sept. 8, 1820, while bathing.

Harlan H. Rice, aged 16, son of Champion B. Rice, was drowned Aug. 18, 1858, at Hoosac Tunnel. He went in company with two others to visit the tunnel while work was in progress there, and it being a very hot day, he went in bathing, just east of the portal of the tunnel, in the Deerfield river, and was drowned. To add to the terrors of the scene, a terrific thunder storm occurred when the party carrying home his body were within two miles of home, accompanied by a very high wind which destroyed trees and buildings. A messenger was sent in advance to break the sad news to the family before the body arrived.

Dea. Ebenezer Fales hung himself at the Town farm, June 30, 1853. He had previously made repeated attempts at self-destruction by pounding his head, cutting his throat, and drowning.

Roswell Longley hung himself Feb. 28, 1846, while confined in an insane asylum.

A Mr. Bassett from Charlemont was once killed in this town by being thrown from his wagon.

Daniel Fletcher, came to Hawley before 1800, settled a little east of where Otis Beals formerly, lived, fell from a wagon and broke his neck.

Jotham King's house and contents were burned in the early years of the town's history.

Theophilus Crosby's house was burned in 1809 or 10.

Warrmer King's sawmill and a large lot of lumber was burned about 1820.

Joseph Merriam, aged 15, son of Rev. Jonathan Grout, was drowned in June, 1823, while playing in the water with a party of other boys.

Otis Longley, a native of Hawley, moved to Lawrence, Kansas, in middle life. He was foully murdered Aug. 23, 1863, at the age of 51, by Quantrell's gang in their raid upon the town. Abbott, in his History of the Civil War, describing the scene, says, "The wife and daughter of a man threw themselves on his body, begging for his life. One of the rebel gang thrust his revolver between them and shot the man. Mrs. Longley since married Dea. Samuel Williams of West Hawley, and died a few years ago. The daughter, Angeline, married Dr. Ashley, a western clergyman.

Leavitt Hallock's tannery and several thousand cords of bark were burned Feb. 11, 1846. The heat from the burning piles of bark was so intense for two days that it was necessary to keep the adjoining buildings wet to prevent their taking fire. This was the most disastrous fire ever occurring in town, and was the cause of reducing a once prosperous hamlet to a place known only in the memories of the past.

The Col. Noah Joy place, including hotel, two barns, and most of their contents were burned in 1865.

Chandler Blanchard's house and barn were burned in Dec. 1880.

Other fires without record of date were Ichabod Hawkes' house, Nathan Clark's house, S. Burt's house, the Jonas King house, occupied by the Larrabee family, the Union schoolhouse, C. W. Fullers store, kept by A. G. Ayres, a house at Fullerville, occupied by a French family, a schoolhouse at West Hawley, P. Starks' shop and sugar house, a sawmill run by Elisha Hunt and Zenas Thayer. The well-remembered flood of Oct. 4, 1869, was very disastrous to property, particularly on Chickley's river, where every bridge was carried away, also Edward Peck's sawmill, and other mills were disabled.

Andrew, a little son of Ziba Pool living at Warriner King's, died Jan. 3, 1829, in consequence of a kernel of pop corn lodging in his throat.

Thomas L., aged 22, son of Gen. Thomas Longley, was drowned July 15, 1843.

About 1827, the body of a Mrs. Town of Plainfield was found in a swamp near the site of a sawmill formerly owned by Phineas Starks. She had wandered away from home in a fit of mental aberration and called at the house of Warriner King, now the Town farm. Amos Griggs then a boy living there, saw her leave the house and pass on up the road, which was the last account her friends could receive of her. A large party of men organized a search and scoured the country for miles around and after several days' search they decided to look one day more and give it up, and on the last day she was found as above stated.

A BEAR STORY.

The events narrated below occurred in 1795 or 6. Aaron Baird was the first man who built a house and lived on what is now the Hawley Town farm. One morning he discovered that a bear had entered his yard and killed one of his best sheep and left it partly devoured near by. He set a trap, baited with the remains of the sheep, attached a heavy clog and awaited the result. The next morning the trap was gone, the trail showing the track of a bear. The news was soon spread and his neighbors turned out to secure the game. Among those joining in the hunt were Capt. Simeon Crittenden and John Stratton, living at Hallockville, about a mile from Mr. Baird's. Most of the men took the precaution to leave their boys at home, but Mr. Stratton allowed his son, a boy of 10 or 12 years of age to go, charging him to keep behind the men, which he did. The party in their search passed by the bear and when the boy came on the bear sprang from his hiding place and caught him, fastening his jaws firmly on his thigh and held him fast. His cries soon made his condition known—but what was to be done? To shoot the bear might kill the boy. No time was to be lost. Mr Crittenden stepped forward and buried an ax in the bear's head, which caused him to release his hold, and the boy was liberated from his terrible condition, his wound bound up and he was carried to his home, where he lay many weeks under the care of Dr. Bryant of Cummington. He nearly bled to death at the time of the accident, and his recovery was a wonderful one, though he lived many years after, but never had a taste for hunting bears. This occurred near where Geo. K. Starks now lives. It might be added that the Simeon Crittenden referred to was grandfather of Charles Crittenden of Hawley, and G. D. Crittenden of Shelburne Falls.

FAMILY RECORDS.

Phineas Scott, b. March 13, 1756, in Whately, was the first Scott in Hawley and settled where his grandson Thaxter now lives. He was the son of David, son of Joseph, son of William, son of Robert, b. about 1600. David Scott possessed many sterling qualities. He was a carpenter, and originated the square rule in lieu of the old "try rule," formerly used for framing. He was also a great hunter. When he died he had 218 descendants living. Phineas Scott m. Rhoda Crafts, Dec. 26, 1776, and moved to Hawley in 1782. (See "Sketches and Incidents.") Children, Patty, b. Dec. 29, 1779, Reuben, b. May 7, 1782, Phineas Jr., b. Oct. 17, 1784, d. Oct. 8, 1808, Rhoda, b. July 7, 1786, Asa, b. Oct. 8, 1788, d. Oct. 22, 1820, Reuben, b. Apr. 11, 1791, d. Dec. 26, 1871, Minerva, b. Sept. 22, 1793, d. June 22, 1822, Calvin, b. Mar. 12 1796, d. Feb. 4, 1860, Luther, b. Aug. 2, 1798.

Children of Reuben and Electa (Harmon) Scott. Martha, b. Feb. 9, 1813, Phineas, b. Sept. 19, 1815, Elijah H. b. Jan. 16, 1819, Reuben, b. Mar. 18, 1823, Saphronia, b. Aug. 29, 1820, Lucius, b. May 26, 1825, Edwin, b. Mar. 29 1827, Saphronia E. b. Jan. 12, 1829, Irena W. b. May 13, 1832.

Children of Luther and Rebecca (Harmon) Scott; Samuel, b. Oct. 9, 1828. Melissa, b. Mar. 10, 1830, Thaxter, b. Mar. 31, 1831, Olive, b. June 6, 1832, Ruth, b. Nov. 20, 1835, Elizabeth, b. June 5, 1838.

Children of Edwin and Ann Eliza (Longley) Scott; George E., b. May 8, 1856, d. Aug. 28, 1860, Florence B. b. May 11, 1861, Frank B. b. Sept. 10, 1855, Carrie L., b. Aug. 11, 1869, d. May 21, 1886.

Edmund Longley, familiarly known as "Squire Edmund," came from Groton, Mass., in 1780, b. Nov. 1, 1746, d. Nov. 29, 1842. His wife, Alice, b. Sept. 13, 1749, d. Feb. 21, 1832. Their children were Thomas, b. Sept. 4, 1774, d. Sept. 22, 1848, Edmund, b. Apr. 11, 1779, d. Aug 18, 1853, Olive, b. June 28, 1781, Rhoda, b. Oct. 20, 1783, d. Sept. 7, 1794. Luther, b. Aug. 16, 1785, d. June 12, 1832, Joshua, b. Aug. 26,

1788, d. Nov. 2, 1851, Calvin, b. April 5, 1791, d .Sept. 10, 1794.

Gen. Thomas Longley m. Martha Arms. Their children were a son, b. Sept. 11, 1805, d. Sept. 24, 1855, Martha A., b. Sept. 30, 1806, d. Jan. 26, 1817, Thomas L. b. July 13, 1803, d. June 4, 1821, Alfred, b. Nov. 10, 1809, Lucretia S., b. Oct. 4, 1811, Mary Ann, b. Nov. 10, 1813 Moses M , b. June 14, 1815, Martha A. 2d, b. June 24, 1817, d. May 11, 1820, Rhoda O., b. March 2, 1819, d. April 28, 1821, Thomas L., b. Feb 15, 1821, d. July 15, 1843, Joseph G., b. May 24, 1823, d. May 4, 1871, HenriettaA., b. July 12, 1826, d. Sept. 9, 1850.

Capt. Edmund Longley m. Olive Field, Oct. 26, 1805. Their children were Edmund, b. Aug. 5, 1806, d. Oct. 28, 1829, Calvin C., b. Jan. 29, 1808, d. Nov. 17, 1825, Elijah F., b. May 13, 1810, Otis, b June 19, 1812, d. Aug. 23, 1833, William F., b. Aug. 6, 1814, Freeman, b. Oct. 19, 1816, Wealthy F., b. July, 13, 1819, Abner T., b. Nov. 26, 1821, Olive W., b. May 16, 1824, Eliza H., b. Sept. 11, 1827.

Luther Longley m. Harriet Shattuck, Jan. 5, 1808. Children, Calvin S., b. Nov. 20, 1809, d. Apr, 12, 1858, Dan, b. Mar. 25, 1812, lived two days, Luther, b. May 5, 1813, d. April 21, 1875, Alice L., b. Aug. 3, '15 d. June 3, 1862, Harriet N., b. July 9, 1818, d. Feb. 5, 1864, Oliver S., b. July 23, 1820, d, March 11, 1876, S. Newell, b. Feb. 7, 1823, d. Dec. 4, 1864, R. Olivia, b. May 13, 1825, m. Uzal Bisdee, Emily L., b. March 2, 1828.

Joshua Longley m. Eliza Hawks. Their children were Roswell, b. Feb. 27, 1813, d. Feb. 28, 1846, Henry A., b. June 5, 1814, Sylvia H. b. Aug. 27, 1815, Olive W., b. July 29, 1817, d. April 22, 1820, L Worcester, b, May 11, 1822, Augustus H., b. Nov.4, 1824, Chalmers P. b. June 30. 1827, Elizabeth, b. Jan. 14, 1831, d. Jan. 27, 1842, Julia A., b. March 11, 1833.

Calvin S. Longley m. Eliza Joy, Oct. 25, 1832. Children, Ann Eliza, b. Apr. 23, 1833, (For her children see the Scott family.) Sylvia H. b. Sept. 30, 1835. m. John H. Bassett, Persis J. b. Sept. 18, 1837, d. Dec. 20. 1837, two sons died in infancy, Carrie E. b. Dec. 15, '42, m. Nathaniel Lampson, June 5, '61, d. Apr. 4, '72, Julia M. b. July 6, '45, Flora A. b. Mar. 10, '54° m. Nathaniel Lampson, Dec. 24, 1872

Oliver S. Longley m. 1st Elizabeth Meekins, 2d Mrs. R. A. Kinney. His children were, Luther, b. May 12, '49, d. Aug, 12, '52, Sarah J. b. Aug. 5, '46, d. Fed. 20, '78, Ella M. b. Aug. 16, '54, d. Apr. 14, '68,

S. Newell Longley m. Maria Bassett, Aug. 20, '49. Children, Alice M. b. Oct. 17, '50, d. Dec. 15, '72, Lizzie A., b. Jan. 23, '53, d. June 21 '59, Abby L., b. July 14, '55, Harriet L., b. Jan. 17, '60.

Luther Longley Jr. m. Elizabeth Mc Dougal in 1842 and had one son, Oscar Eugene .

Elijah F. Longley had two children, died young.

Joseph Longley, known as "Master Joe," came from Groton, in 1780. He died July 8, 1836, aged 92. His wife Elizabeth d. Feb. 1, 1797. He m. Mrs. Lucy Shattuck, Dec. 13, 1797, she d. May 20, 1834. Children, Jonas, b. Oct. 25, 1793, d. Sept. 14, 1794, Sally, b. Aug. 28, 1795, d. Nov. 10, 1802, Jonas P. d. June 27, 1799, Lyman, b. Mar. 14, 1801, Olive, b. Jan. 20, 1803, m. Ira Holden, Oct. 7, 1828, Calvin, b. Jan. 4, 1805, d. May 26, 1805, Sally 2d, b. May 5, 1806, m. C. W. Stanard, Nov 21, 1826, d, Jan. 12, '76, James S. b. Mar. 4, 1808, Caroline, b. Sept, 24, 1810, m. J. G. Field, d. '72, Zachariah, b. Apr. 7, 1814.

Zimri Longley and Lucy, had Loren, b. Mar. 22, 1794, and two others who died in infancy. His wife d. July 31, 1805, and he afterward m. Esther Wood.

Loren Longley m. Thankful Tripp, and had Lucy, b. May 5, 1819, Elizabeth, b. Apr. 28, 1821, d. July 8, 1822, Lorenzo, b. Oct. 16, 1824, Elizabeth, b. Apr. 30, 1826.

Jonas P. Longley m. Almira Crittenden, Dec. 2, 1818. Children, Sally, b Sept. 25, 1820, Olive, b. Sept. 5, 1822, Lyman, b. Aug. 30, 1824, Eliza, b. Apr. 7, 1827, m. Elbridge King.

James Sullivan Longley m. Saphronia Miles, Dec. 9, 1828. Children, Lewis, b. Dec. 24, 1830, m. Laura Beals, Luther, b. Apr. 14, 1832, d. May 14, 1832, Edwin, b. May 22, 1835.

Thomas King, b. Jan. 25, 1729, came from Brimfield to Hawley, May 3, 1772, and located where his son Ezra lived and died. He marrried Abigail Warriner, by whom he had Thomas, Jonas, b. Feb 13, 1754, Amos and Abigail, twins, b. March 12, 1758, Jotham, b. July 16, 1760, Titus, Betsey and Daniel. His wife d. and he m. Mercy Vincent, b. Jan. 20, 1744, by whom he had John, b. Aug. 5, 1782, Ezra, b. Aug. 1, 1784.

Children of Jonas and Abigail (Leonard) King; Hannah, b. Dec. 14, 1783, m. Samuel Wheeler, Jonas, b. July 29, 1792. He was the distinguished missionary to Palestine and Greece.

Amos King m. June 29, 1786, Esther Robinson, b. Jan. 30, 1767, Their children were Warriner, b. May 28, 1787, m. Elizabeth Crowell, d. Feb. 27, 1877, Jerusha, b. Nov. 25, 1788, m. Ezra King, d. May 29, 1882, Esther, b. Dec. 5, 1790 m. 1st Ziba Fenton, 2d Lemuel Lombard, in 1837, Lydia, b. Oct 2, 1792, m. Chester F. Griggs, d Feb. 24, 1853, Minerva, b. Sept. 27 1794, m. Willard Nash and moved to Ohio, Abigail, b. Apr. 24, 1796, d. July 29, 1800, Roana, b. Apr. 22, 1798, m. Dennis Bangs and removed to Central New York, still living, Abigail 2d, b. July 25, 1800 m. 1st Jeremiah Taylor, 2d. Sumner Barton, still living Amos Jr., b. Aug 9, 1802, Joanna, b. Aug. 10, 1804, d. Sept. 19, 1806, Samantha, b. Jan. 1, 1807, m. Theron Skeels and went to Ohio.

Children of Jotham King; Clarissa, b. Dec. 6, 1786, Sally, b. June 29, 1789, Experience, b. April 16, 1793.

Children of Ezra and Jerusha King; Hiram, b. Aug. 21, 1806, d. 1885, Mercy, b. June 7, 1808, m. George Rice, lives at North Adams, Joanna, b. Jan. 15, 1810, Chloe R. b. Jan. 26, 1812, m. 1st Elisha Ford, 2d, Merritt Jones, Esther, b. March 14, 1814, m. James Ferry and lives at Stafford, Ct., Olive B., b. March 4, 1816, m. Edward Coope, Ezra, b. Dec. 20, 1817, John Warriner, b. Nov. 15, 1819, Sylvia, b. Oct. 26, 1821, Abigail, b. Feb. 20, 1823, m. Abner Longley and res. in Washington, D. C., Mahaleth, b. Oct. 8, 1824, m. Nelson Joy, Jerusha, m. Henry Joy.

Capt. John King m. Electa Shattuck, July 3, 1817. Children, Electa, b. March 6, 1820, Thera S., b. Oct. 3, 1821, John Vincent, b. June 30, 1823, a daughter, b. July 24, 1825, Mary, 1827.

Timothy Baker came from Sunderland or Conway to Hawley in 1772. He was b. May 15, 1748, and was the son of Noah, b. 1719, son of John, b. 1680, son of Timothy, b. 1647, son of Edward, who came from England in 1630. He m. Abigail Kibbe, b. May 19, 1750. Children, Rufus, b. May 7, 1773, Julia, b. Nov. 22, 1774, Hollister, b. Feb. 4, 1777, Harmena, b. Oct. 11, 1779, Abigail, b. Dec. 31, 1782, Timothy, b. Feb. 10, 1784, Ephraim, b. May 11, 1786, Sarah, b. Jan. 10, 1788, Clarissa, b May 24, 1790, Sophia, b. Oct. 3, 1793, m. 1st Edmund Hawks, 2d Jonathan Fuller.

. Hollister Baker m. Rebecca C. owell, Oct. 22, 1799. Their children were Horace, b. Dec. 11, 1800, m. Apr. 13, 1826, Mary Ann Curtis, Harvey, b. Apr. 30, 1803, m. June '14, 27, Ann Eliza Carter, Rebecca, b. Mar. 20, 1805, m. Dec. 11, 1827, Freeman Atkins, Ephraim, b. Nov. 7, 1807, had three wives, moved to Wisconsin and became wealthy, Harriet b. Feb. 19, 1812, m. Mar. '37, John W. Hawkes, Roswell, b. Mar, 16, '17, m. Oct. 1839, Bathsheba Carter, Charles, b. Apr. 4, 1820, m. May 28, 1848, Wealthy W. Shattuck, Ereda, b. Oct. 1822, m. Nathan Howes, Aug 4, 1842.

Children of Horace and Mary Ann (Curtis) Baker. Eliza, b. June 12, 1827, m. June 17, '50, Edmund Beals. Henry, b. Mar. 21, 1829, m. Lucy Hills, Hollister, b. Oct. 12, 1831, d. '45, Tyler, b. Nov. 11, 1833, m. Betsey Russell, 1866, James, b. Feb, 6. 1838, m. Harriet Cook, 1866, Nathan, b. Oct. 5, 1841, m. Mary J. Carey, 1862.

Children of Harvey and Ann Eliza (Carter) Baker; Dennis W, b. Jan. 16, 1829, m. Lucretia Vincent, March 18, 1855, d. in Charlemont, Bridgman C., b. Sept. 3, 1830, removed to Lamoille, Ill., and died there, Silas D. b. Aug. 18, 1832, lived two years, Charles F., b. Apr. 27, 1834, d. March 20, 1844, Lucius T., b. Apr. 25, 1836, d. Nov. 30, '53, Noah, b. Apr. 3, 1838, killed at the siege of Port Hudson, June 14, '63, Allen C. b. Feb. 3, 1840, Mariette, b. June 3, 1841, m. C. B. Mayhew, Angeline, b. June 3, 1843, Preston, b. June 15, '45, resides in Charlemont, Martha, b. Oct. 23, 1848, Franklin, b. Oct. 14, 1850. Eliza, b. Aug. 21 1853.

Children of Roswell and Bathsheba (Carter) Baker; Ereda, b. Jan. 4, 1841, m. Stephen B. Buddington, Edwin, b. Jan. 18, 1843, druggist at Shelburne Falls.

Rufus Baker m. Olive Hall, Dec. 24, 1795. Their children were, Austin, b. Aug. 20. 1797, Rufus, b. Feb. 8, 1802, m. Rebecca Rice, Olive, b. Apr. 27, 1804, m. Andrew Ford. Achsah, b. Jan. 10, 1806, m. John K. Crosby, Timothy, b. Oct. 1807, m. Maria Sears, res. in Adams, Octavia, b. Aug. 5, 1809, Thomas K., b. Nov. 15, 1811, res. in Springfield, Joel, b. Nov. 17, 1813, m. Mary Dunham, Phebe, b. June 17, 1816, d. Dec. 4, 1828, Abigail, K. b. Apr. 24, 1819, d. Aug. 26, 1848.

Children of Joel and Mary (Dunham) Baker; Rufus, b. Aug. 30, 1839, Nathan B., b. July 20, 1841, res. in Savoy. He was a member of Co. E, 52d Mass. Regt. in the Civil War.

Jonathan Fuller is believed to have come from Lenox about 1785, and located where his son Jonathan recently lived. He was b. Aug. 23, 1757, Anna, his wife, b. Mar. 29, 1764. Their children were Hannah, b. Apr. 1, 1786, Daniel, b. Jan 22, 1788, Hollis, b. Nov. 20, 1789, Jonathan, b. May 1, 1792, d. Dec. 18, 1882, Anna, b. May 16, 1794, Orin, b. Apr. 28, 1796, Shubael, b. July 12, 1798, m. —— Robinson, moved to Cicero, N. Y., Bathsheba, b. March 9, 1801, m. Phillip Perry, Ira. m. 1st Miss Leonard, 2d, Mrs. Abigail Elmer, passed the most of his life in Savoy, now lives in Hawley, William, m. — Miles, removed to Ashfield.

Jonathan Fuller Jr. m. Lucinda Leonard, b. March 9, 1801, and had, Clark W. b. Nov 27, 1822, Eliza Ann. b. March 4, 1824, Bathsheba, b. Aug. 8, 1826, m. 1st Wells Ayres, 2d, Levi Hawkes, Clark W. 2d, b. April 1, 1829, m. Sarah Larkins, res. in Boston. His wife d. and he m. Mrs, Sophia Hawkes, Dec. 17, '35 by whom he had Lorinda H, b. Sept. 20, 1836, m. Oct 10 1855, John C. Beals, and d. Nov. 27, 1858.'

Children of Wells and Bathsheba (Fuller) Ayres; Flora, b. June 14, 1851, d. young, Anna, b. May 18, 1853, m. Albert E. Marsh, resides in Northampton, Cary C., b, Aug. 8, 1860.

Abisha Rogers came from the eastern part of the state and settled in Bozrah. He was b. Feb. 1, 1762. Betsey, his wife was b. June 28, 1765, their children were, Cynthia, b. Sept. 2, 1786, Micah,b. Aug. 22, 1788, Sally, b. Nov. 27, 1790, Molly, b. Mar, 15, 1793.

Elihu Russell, b. July 30, 1768, Miriam his wife b. Dec. 10, 1775, their children were, Levi, b. Jan. 13, 1791, Betty, b. Apr. 4,1793, Elihu, b. Mar. 30, 1795.

Wm. Farnsworth, b. Nov. 15, 1766, Delight, his wife b. Mar. 6, 1768, Children, Aaron, b. Aug. 21, 1791, Tirzah, b. Mar. 30, 1793.

Daniel Burt came, 1771, settled east of the old burying-ground, at this house the first Thanksgiving was held, b. Sept. 19, 1730, Margaret; his wife was b. Dec. 27, 1727, Daniel, their son, b. Mar. 2, 1764.

Other children of Abisha Rogers; Abia, b. Aug. 22, 1788, Ellis, b. Feb. 8, 1795, Nathaniel, b, Jan. 29, 1797, Betsey, b. Apr. 22, 1799, m. Atherton Hunt Mar. 30, 1826, Elias, b. Feb. 10, 1801, Simeon, b. Apr. 25, 1803, Electa, b. Sept, 26, 1806, Moses, b. Apr. 12, 1809, Sarah H. b. Feb. 7, 1811.

Ebenezer Hall came early and settled where Sylvester Rice lives. He was b. Mar. 21, 1759, Lydia, his wife b. Sept. 2, 1760. Children, Elizabeth, b. Nov. 2, 1783, Keziah, b. July 28, 1785, m. Nov. 29, 1810, Rufus Hall, Lydia, b. Mar 30, 1787, Ebenezer, b. May 27, 1788, Esther, b. July 4, 1787, d. Sept. 18, 1866, John, b. May 9, 1793, m. Oct. 1818, Ruth Bangs, Polly, b. Oct. 8, 1796, Achsah, b. Dec. 16, 1799, Samuel, b. Sept, 11, 1802, m. 1st Azubah Howes, 2d Deborah Carter, d. Jan. 26 1877. Their children were Ebenezer, b. Aug. 22, 1830, d. in Ill. A daughter b. Mar. 7, 1832, Samuel M. b. Jan. 9, 1841, killed in the war, Emily A. b. Oct. 23,1842, m. Moses M. Mantor, Apr. 23, 1861, Thomas A. b. July 2, 1844, d. in the army. Lewis J. b. May 19 1846, Julia A. b. Mar. 21, 1848, m. Charles Crittenden, June 22, 1870, d. May 22, '82, Mary E. b. Sept. 8, 1850, Laura J., b. Mar. 20, 1856.

Children of Ebenezer Hall, Jr., Thomas A., b. Sept. 2, 1813, Washburne b. July 25, 1815, Sophia, b. Oct. 6, 1817, Moses Smith, b. Mar. 1, 1824.

Silas Parker, b. Sept. 5, 1770, Sarah, his wife, b. June 17, 1768, their children were Cephas, b. Dec. 12, 1788, Phebe, b. Apr. 22, 1789, Silas, b. Oct. 2, 1790, Sibel, b. Nov. 2, 1792.

Abraham Parker came from Whately, was one of the early settlers, b. May 30, 1751, m. April 8, 1783, Abigail Ingram, b. Aug. 12, 1753. Of their children but two grew to maturity, Abraham, b. Dec. 7, 1792, Samuel, b. Dec. 16, 1798.

Abraham Parker Jr. stayed on the old homestead, m. Achsah Howes, b. Dec. 27, 1784. Children, Lois, b. Aug. 14, 1812, m. Leonard Marsh Lucretia, b. July 4, '14, Betsey S., b. Aug. 22, '16, m. William Ingram, Chapman H., b. July 3, 1819, m. Esther Gurney, d. Dec. 15, 1863, Lucretia B., b. Jan. 5, 1822, James M., b. Feb. 25, 1824, Abbie I., b. Jan. 17, 1826, m. Elijah Gibbs, Abraham 3d, b. April 3, 1831, m. Ellen S. Phipps, resides in Amherst.

James M. Parker, m. Orilla P. Ingram, Oct, 4, 1848, and had Alvan H. b. May 25, 1852, Herbert M. b. Aug. 13, 1861, and had two daughters died young. His wife d. June 29, 1886, and he m. Mrs. Mary Brayman, Nov. 4, '71, by whom he had Wilber E. b. '72, Charles S. b. '74.

Nathaniel Parker, b. Dec. 14, 1741, Martha, his wife b. Sept. 14, '41, their children were James, b. Oct. 10, 1766, William, b. Jan. 19, 1769, Katharine, b. Aug. 11, 1771, Mary, Oct. 10, 1776, Nathaniel, b. May 19, 1779, Esther, b. Oct. 16, 1781, Bani, b. Apr. 29, 1781, Abel, b. Mar. 5, 1788.

Asa Parker b. Feb. 13, 1773, Elizabeth, his wife, b. Aug. 16, 1760, Children, Emma, b. March 19, 1793, Phila, b. Dec. 10, 1794, Betsey, b. April 17, 1797, Thiora. b. Jan. 11, 1799.

Zenas Parker, son of William and Mehitable, b. July 11, 1796, Mehitable, b. June 16, 1799, Florilla, b. Sept. 27, 1801, William, b. June 25, 1804, Calvin, b. May 10, 1809, Lois, b. March 4, 1811, Lydia, b. July 4, 1813, Elenzer, b. March 20, 1798.

Samuel Hitchcock was one of the first four families which came to Hawley, in 1771, and located near the old burying ground. He was b. Dec. 16, 1744, his wife, Thankful, b. Sept. 1, 1746. Their children were Ethan, b. Oct. 18, 1773, the first birth in town. He lived to a very advanced age, and died at Shelburne Falls, Samuel, b. Apr. 6, 1775, Ruth b. July 8, 1776, Pliny, b. Nov. 20, 1779, Urbane, Dec. 1, 1781, became a Congregational clergyman, Thankful, b. June 24, 1783, Asenath, b. Oct. 15, 1784, Erastus, b. Oct. 18, 1787, Eli, b. Feb. 2, 1789.

Children of Ethan Hitchcock; Clarissa, b. Feb. 23, 1794, Rhoda, b. Jan. 23, 1796, Quartus, b. Dec. 31, 1797, Eu, b. Nov. 27, 1800, Asenath b. Aug. 19, 1803, Rosamond, b. Apr. 9, 1809, Ethan, b. Dec. 10, 1812.

Arthur Hitchcock came early and settled where his grandson, Joseph A. lives. He was b. Sept. 5, 1751, Lucy, his wife, b. Jan. 8, 1759, their children were Lucy, b. Oct. 31, 1779, Arthur, b. Mar. 3, 1783, Lucinda, b. Jan. 1, 1785, Sarah, b. Feb. 25, 1787, Lois, b. Sept, 6, 1789, Simeon, b. Jan. 28. 1792, Nancy, Apr, 7, 1794, Polly, b. Oct. 6, 1796, Heman, b. Sept. 25, 1799, m. May 1827, Elizabeth Thayer, b. July 5, 1804,

Their children were Joseph A. b. July 15, 1828, m. May 30, 1861. Emily M. Barnes, Emily T. b. July 26, 1832, lives in Vt. Juliette, b. June 18, 1838, lives in Conway, Oramel C. b. Mar. 26, 1841. Children of Joseph A. and Emily (Barnes) Hitchcock. A daughter b. July 26, '64, lived five weeks, Clara E. b. Aug. 10, 1865, Preston W. b. Nov. 18, 1872, Cora A. b. Jan. 11, 1877.

Zenas Bangs came from Dennis about 1786, and settled where Francis W. Atkins lives. He was b. May 3, 1763, Ruth, his wife, b. Sept. 25, 1762. Children, Orrin, b. May 28, 1786, Rebecca, b. Dec, 8, 1787, Allen b. June 27, 1789, Zenas, b. March 25, 1791, David, b. Sept. 25, 1792, Dennis, b. June 25, 1764, m. Roana King, Lewis, b. July 18, 1798, Ruth, b. June 6, 1799, m. John Hall, Luke, b. May 11, 1801, Mary, b. July 16, 1804.

Zenas Bangs Jr. m. Nabby Crosby, Oct. 23, 1806. Children, Samuel L. b. July 8, 1808, Nabby, b. May 1, 1810.

Joseph Bangs, b. July 5, 1757, Desire, his wife, b. Aug. 24, 1760. Children, Phebe, b. Sept. 5, 1779, Joseph. b. Oct. 10, 1783, Desire, b. Dec. 9, 1785, Sarah, b. Jan. 6, 1788, Polly, b. Feb. 28, 1790, Jonathan, b. Feb. 9, 1792, Sabra, b. Feb. 10, 1794, Olive, b. June 8, 1796, Washington, b. Oct. 16, 1798, Freeman S. b. July 11, 1804.

Elijah Marsh came to Hawley before 1800, and settled half a mile east of the Town farm He was the sixth generation from John Marsh, who came from England and settled in Hartford, Ct., in 1639. He was b. in Conway, Feb. 8, 1777, m. Tamzin Howes, May 27, 1800, d. May 1814. Their children were Emily b Aug. 5, 1801, d. May 1810, Loron, b. Nov. 9, 1803, m. Julia Rice, now living in Riceville Pa. Sylvanus, b. May 16, 1805, d. Aug.19, 1844, Luther, b. May 30, 1809, m. Susan Breed of Hawley, Aug. 22, 1832, Tamzin, b. June 28, 1812, removed to Wayne, Pa. m. Philander Miller. Elijah's wife d. and he m. 2d Elizabeth Alden, Sept. 8, 1814, the sixth generation from John Alden who came over in the Mayflower in 1620. Their children were Martha A. b. May 31, 1815, d. June 10, 1837, Elijah Jr. b. Apr. 23, 1817, d. Apr. 27, 1834, Emily, b. Apr. 20, 1820,d. Feb. 14, 1844, Joseph, b. May 26, 1822, removed to Whately, m. July 20, 1848, Mary E. Jenny, who d. Nov. 28, 1848, m. 2d, June 6, 1860, Mary C. Parsons. He now resides in Northampton, and is a bookseller. (We are indebted to him for these records.) Jonathan, b. July 27, 1824, m. Harriet L. Miller, resides in Corry, Pa.

Ephraim Marsh lived in the old sixth school district. His children were Proctor, b. Nov. 9, 1795, became a Methodist minister, Mary, b. Sept. 8, 1798, Ephraim, b. Nov. 17, 1801, Wilder, b. March 20, 1804, Hannah, b. March 16, 1806, Polly, b. Jan.11, 1808, Leonard, b. May 15 1811, Polly, 2d, b. Feb. 14, 1813, Emily, b. July 16, 1814, Abner, b. Jan. 12, 1816, m. Loe Rice, Theodore, b. Mar. 30, 1818, Susanna, b. Nov. 22, 1819.

Leonard Marsh remained where his father lived until a few years ago, when he removed to Amherst. He m. Lois Parker; his children were Jane A., b. Sept. 28, 1834, Theodore C., b. Mar. 30, 1838, Albeert E. b. Dec. 20, 1840, m. Anna Ayres and resides in Northampton, Lucretia, b. June 12, 1843, Joel W., b. Jan. 20, 1846, Achsah S., b. Jan. 17, 1858.

Calvin Oakes came early and settled in Pudding Hollow. His children were William, b. May 26, 1788, Calvin, b. May 26, 1790, Cary, b. Sept. 12, 1792, Isaac, b. June 10, 1795, became a Congregational minister, David, b. June 21, 1797, Caleb, b. June 29, 1801.

Children of William Oakes, Geo. W., b. Oct. 23, 1813, Eliza, b. Mar. 12, 1815.

John Oakes b. May 7, 1769, Mercy, his wife, b. March 13, 1773, their children were Abigail, b. July 24, 1797, Sally, b. June 1, 1799, John, b. March 26, 1804, Joel, b. Feb. 1806, Avery, b. Jan. 20, 1808, Luther, b. April 7, 1810, Levi, b. Sept. 23, 1811.

Timothy Worthington, b. Jan. 2, 1757, Olive, his wife, b. Dec. 2, 1763 Children, Samuel, b. March 4, 1789, John, b. May 28, 1791, Timothy, b. Jan. 5, 1794, Sally, b. June 28, 1796, Elisha, b Oct. 19, 1797, Ansel, b. Nov. 4, 1801, Ansel 2d, b. Dec. 25, 1804.

Henry Look, b. May 19, 1763, Hepzibah, his wife b. Oct. 19, 1764, their children were Marshall, b. Nov. 8, 1786, Roxana, b. Apr. 14, 1789, Betty, b. July 4, 1791, Mordecia, b. Dec. 1, 1793.

Rufus Sears, known as Dea. Sears, when a boy of 11 years came from Dennis with Joseph Bangs soon after 1780, and lived to a very advanced age. (See Sketches and Incidents.) His wife's name was Priscilla, and their children were Vienna, b. Jan. 23, 1795, Nathaniel, b. Aug. 3, '96, Priscilla, b. March 25, 1798, Daniel, b. Jan. 31, 1800, Rufus, 2d b. Dec. 23, 1803, Anthony, b. Aug. 18, 1805, Priscilla, b. Mar. 3, 1807, Maria, b. Apr. 10, 1806, m. Timothy Baker, resides in Adams, Frederick H. b. June 25,1811, stayed on the old homestead, Benjamin, b. Mar. 15, 1814. He made edge tools at one time in Williamsburg, and died at a recent date.

Anthony Sears lived at Fullerville, m. Lovina Sprague, May 4, 1828. Their children were Rufus, b. March 15, 1829, d. Dec. 27, 1850, at Farmington, Ct. His remains were brought home and buried at West Hawley. In connection with his funeral, Jan. 5, 1851, Rev. John Eastman delivered a half-century sermon, which was published in pamphlet form, by request of a number of parishioners. Jane M. b. Jan. 16, 1833, m. Joseph R. Vining, d. in early life, Lewis E. b. June 7, 1838, m. Lucy Starks, and resides in Plainfield, Maria, b. Nov. 3, 1842, d. in early life, Edwin, lives on the old homestead.

Frederick H. Sears lives on the old homestead, m. Mar. 3, 1836, Rebecca Sears. Their children were Henry F. b. Dec. 25, 1836, graduate of Amherst, now a teacher in Boston. Mary E. b. May 28, 1839, was once an eminent teacher, Freeman B. b. May 10, 1842, Harriet M. b. Apr. 15, 1850, Amelia I. b. Oct. 7, 1851, Chas. F. b. May 4, 1856, and lives with his parents.

Alvan Sears came from Dennis before 1800, and settled on West Hill. He was b. Sept. 26, 1775, Bethiah Howes, his wife, b. Nov. 5, 1777. Their children were Seth, b. July 27, 1801, the oldest native of the town living there, Alvan, b. Jan. 8, 1804, Abigail b, Jan. 9, 1806, m. 1st Horace Elmer, 2d Ira Fuller, Edmund, b. Mar. 26, 1808, Joshua. b. July 19, 1809, Urbane, b. Aug. 2, 1813, Vienna, b. Apr. 22, 1816, lives at West Hawley, Desire, b. July 22, 1819, Edmund 2d b. May 22, 1822.

Urbane Sears remained in West Hawley till the time of his death, which occurred April 6, 1875. He m. Mrs. Tryphosa Hawkes, Apr. 18, 1838. Their children were Martha T., b. May 22, 1839, m. Wills Vincent and res. in Hawley, Edmund H., b. Nov. 2, 1841, d. in the army, Ella C., b. Oct. 18, 1849, m. Lewis W. Temple, Sept. 12, 1871, res. in Hawley, George W., b. May 18, 1855, m. Jennie H. Houston, Oct. 28, 1879, and lives on the homestead with his mother, Clara B., b. Apr. 29, 1857, m. and lives in Deerfield.

Rowland Sears came from Dennis about 1786 and settled on the north line of the town, where Lewis W. Temple lives. His son Benjamin succeeded him on the same farm. His children were Lydia b. Oct. 25, 1813, Rebecca, b. Nov. 5, 1815, m Frederick H. Sears, Harriet, b. Jan. 18, 1818, m. Rodolphus Hawkes, Mary, b. Apr. 19, 1820, Benjamin, b. Apr. 16, 1822. He also succeeded his father and grandfather on the homestead, m. Louisa Atkins, Oct. 10, 1848, and d. Feb. 11, 1870. leaving no children. Elizabeth, b. Apr. 22, 1824.

Alden Sears was b. in Barnstable, July 23, 1774, came to Hawley in Mar. 1795,. He m. Sarah Crosby, Nov. 19, 1801. Their children were Ansel, b. May 25, 1803, Hirah, b. May 25, 1805, Oliver, b. Jan. 22, 1807, Joshua, b. Sept. 18, 1808, Alden, b. May 17, 1810, Sarah, b. Apr. 29, 1812, Ebenezer, b June 15, 1815, m. Cordelia Fales. Children, Albert F. b. Mar. 10, 1840, m. Sarah A. Williams and has a daughter Edith b. Sept. 16, 1875, James F. b. Feb. 9, 1845.

Children of Rowland and Persis Sears; Thankful, b. May 31, 1806, Persis, b. Mar. 1, 1809, Rowland, b. July 20, 1811, Mercy, b. May 8, 1813. Rowland, b. Sept. 16, 1815, Joseph, b. May 28, 1818, Sylvester, b. May. 6, 1821,

Sylvester Sears m. Persis Hall, Sept. 17, 1812. Children, Olive, b. July 22, 1817, Emily, b. June 17, 1819.

Levi Holden was b. in Shirley, Mass., in 1767. He went to Langdon, N. H., m. and buried a wife there, by whom he had two sons, Ira and Joeseph. His 2d marriage was Jan. 9, 1800, to Mary Longley. His children by this marriage were Lydia, b. Apr. 16, 1804, Elizabeth, b. Aug. 6, 1806, Levi, b. June 2, 1807, the first Holden b. in Hawley. Mary, b. June 10, 1809, Dorothy, b. Jan. 28, 1811, Olive, b. Oct. 24, 1812, Lucy, P. b. July 30, 1814, Jonas, b. May 30, 1816.

Ira Holden m. Olive Longley, Oct. 7, 1824. Children, Olive, b. July 6, 1825, Henry A. b. June 30, 1827, resides in Hawley. Cooley L. b. Mar. 16, 1829. Olive, 2d b. June 3, 1831,˙ Asa, b. Feb. 23, 1833, m. Martha E. Hunt. res. in Hawley. Freeman, b. July 31, 1837, Eliza E, b. July 31, 1840, Francis, b. Sept. 3, 1843.

Levi Holden Jr. m. Annie Joy, Oct. 6, 1835. Their children were Ellen A. b. Apr. 5, 1838, m. Henry Clark, res. in Hawley. Merrick J. b. May '40, m. Rebecca Mason. res. in Adams. Eliza L. b. Aug. 15, '43, m. H. W. Stockwell, Charles N. b. Sept. 20, '47, res. in Plainfield, Frank b. Dec. 31, 1856. His wife Annie, d, Jan. 17, 1857, and he m. 2d Mrs. Lucy S. Bennett, Dec. 2, 1858. He d. Aug. 23, 1886.

Elisha L. Clark removed to Hawley, Apr. 9, 1811, He was b. Sept, 8, 1786, m. Mary W. Allis, June 14, 1810, d. July 19, 1862. Children, Samuel A. b. Apr. 24, 1812, lives in Hawely. Elijah D. b. Dec, 22, '15, d. Jan. 21. 1816, Lucius L. b. Nov. 29, 1816, d. Dec. 15, 1884, Elisha

L., b. June 1, 1818, d. Aug. 9, 1851, Thomas D., Sept. 18, 1815 d. Apr. 25, 1871, Jonathan G. b. Mar. 22, 1829, d. Nov. 8, 1860, Tyler T. b. Nov. 13, 1834, d. May 16, 1860.

Samuel A. Clark m. Clarissa Williams of Ashfield, b. Apr. 5, 1817. Their children were Albert B. b. Nov. 24, 1838, served in the 10th Regt. in the civil war, lives in Hawley, Mary A. b. June 1 1841, George D. b. July 19, 1843, d. Sept. 3, 1863, Elisha L. b. Sept. 6, 1845, Samuel A. b. Sept. 17, 1847, Clara A. b. Jan. 11, 1850, Tyler T. b. Nov 20, 1852. Samuel A. Clark m. 2d, Mrs. Lucy W. Packard, June 16, 1853.

Phineas Clark, b. Aug. 20, 1751, Jemima, his wife, b. Mar. 1741. Children, Rufus, b. May 2, 1786, Moses, b. Apr. 23, 1788, Alpheus, b. Oct. 22, 1790, Amasa, b. Dec. 21, 1792, Sylvester, b. Mar. 20, 1796, Clarissa, b. Apr. 10, 1798, Jemima, b. Mar. 11, 1801, Sylvia, b. Nov. 15, 1803, Phineas, b. Aug. 10, 1806.

Joseph Howes, b. May 21, 1770, m. Nov. 16, 1808, Elizabeth Sears, b. Dec. 27, 1781. Their children were Rowland, b. Nov. 26, 1809, Joseph Jr., b. Jan. 23, 1811, Mercy, b. Feb. 18, 1812, Henry, Nov. 9, 1813 Franklin, b. Nov. 28, 1816, Elizabeth, b. Jan. 16, 1818, Elijah B., b. June, 1822, m. Mary Jane Simons, and lives in Hawley.

Henry Howes m. June 1836, Lucy A. Simons, and lives in Cheshire. Their children were Lucy A., b. May 6, 1838, m. Frank Mason, Lovina b. Feb. 4, 1840, m. Charles N. Harlow, and lives in Northampton, Wealthy L. b. Jan. 13, 1842, Augusta M. b. Apr. 21, 1846, William H. b. Mar. 14, 1848, lives with his parents, Edgar, b. March 8, 1850, Fannie, b. Nov. 13, 1852, Charles, b. Feb. 28, 1854.

Children of Edmund and Abiah Howes; Roswell F. b. Aug. 18, 1815, Cynthia, b. Mar. 2, 1817, Fanny W. b. Nov. 5, 1818, Rosamond H. b. Dec. 30, 1820, Henry N. b. Mar. 23, 1823.

Rev. Anson Dyer m. Mercy Howes, Aug. 1, 1833. Children, Elizabeth, b. July 10, 1834, m. Chester Elmer, Mercy A. b. Oct. 14, 1836, Joseph, May 20,1838, Benjamin F. b. May 15, 1841, Harriet A. b. June 11, '43.

John Vincent m. Lucretia Howes and came to Hawley about 1828, where he lived till his death, March 4, 1873. He was prominent and influential in public affairs, held all the highest offices in the gift of the town, was for a long time a Justice of the Peace, and for several terms represented his town and district in the State Legislature. His children were Eliza A., b. July 10 1828, m. Amos Stetson, Willis, b. Dec. 1, 1829, m. Martha T. Sears, lives at the homestead, Lucretia, b. Aug. 26, 1831, m. Dennis W. Baker, Morris, b. Mar. 23. 1833, is a farmer at Milan, Mich., Mark H. b. July 20, 1834, m. Emma A. Brackett, lives at West Hawley, Sarah S. b. Mar. 13, 1837, Albert, served in the 37th Regt. in the war, was several times promoted, and came home with a captain's commission, now a travelling salesman for agricultural tools at Sterling, Ill, Flora A. b. Dec. 31, 1846, m. T. M. Carter of Williamsburg.

HISTORY OF HAWLEY.

Nathan Vincent, brother of John, m. Sarah Curtis, had one son, Isaac C., b. Mar. 2, 1844, m. Delia Carter, and lives in West Hawley.

Children of Joshua Vincent; Joel, b. Aug. 8, 1822, Esther, b. Jan. 28, 1824, Thomas, b. Nov. 18, 1825, Joshua, b. March 8, 1827, Mary E., b. Jan. 24, 1829, Micajah H., b. Nov. 7, 1830, Rebecca, b. Dec. 20, 1834.

Warham Stiles, b. July 25, 1772, m. Sarah Nelson, b. Feb. 23, 1781. They came from Westfield to Hawley a little before 1800, and settled on West Hill. Their children were Rowland, b. July 8, 1800, Warren, b. May 19, 1802, Garner, b. May 16, 1804, settled in Hawley, d. Mar. 28, 1871, Alva, b. July 5, 1806, Sarah, b. Apr. 6, 1808, Sarah 2d b. March 12, 1810, Martin, b. May 17, 1812, lived at North Adams, Roxey, b. Mar. 23, 1814, Nelson, b. Mar. 23, 1816, Horace, b. July, 10, 1819, Tirzah, b. Apr; 27, 1821, m. Sanderson E. Carter and settled in Hawley, Polly, b. Feb. 23, 1823, Lucy, b. Feb. 28, 1827, m. Chas. Peck, Rowland, b. Apr. 15, 1831, lives on the homestead.

Children of Garner Stiles; William, Harriet, John, b. Jan. 8, 1835, Harvey, b. Mar. 8, 1836, Fanny, m. Alonzo F. Turner, Mary J., m. Charles Anthony, Cornelia, b. Aug. 13, 1844, m. Samuel T. Horton, d. July 8, 1886.

Rev. Jonathan Grout m. Polly Taylor of Buckland, Sept. 27, 1795. Their children were Polly, b. May 22, 1798, Saphronia, b. July 12, 1800. Jonathan. b. Mar. 26, 1802, Samuel T. b. Apr. 14, 1804, lived in Hawley until a few years ago when he removed to Deerfield and lives with his three daughters, Esther, b. Aug. 7, 1806, Joseph Merriam, b. July 31, 1808, drowned, June, 1823, Henry T. b. Aug. 7, 1810, d. June 12, 1886, Sarah H. b. Oct. 6, 1812.

Samuel Taylor Grout m. May 9, 1826, Laura Joy. Their children were Laura Alfreda, b. April 13, 1827, m. 1st Justin B. Warriner, 2d Christopher A. Stebbins, lives at Deerfield, Thaxter P., b. Dec. 2, 1829, Hannah J., b. Mar 20, 1832, Mary P., b, Aug. 13, 1834, m. ——Warfield, lives at Deerfield, and has the care of Memorial Hall, Jonathan, b. Feb. 22, 1837, Lucy E. b. Feb. 3, 1839, m. Henry Childs, station agent on the Connecticut River railroad, Jonathan 2d, b. Dec. 21 1842, Moses W., b. Dec. 26, 1845, Henry T. b. Dec. 25, 1850.

Joseph Easton b. May 23. 1767, Mary, his wife, b. June 7, 1766. Children, Mary, b. Sept. 8, 1786, John, b. Dec. 8, 1790, James, b. April 2, 1795, Joseph, b. Sept. 15, 1797, Justus, b. July 30, 1799, Alexander, b. Sept. 25, 1801, Orlando, b. July 8, 1803, Luman, b. April 23, 1806.

Elisha Wells, b. July 30, 1747, Emma his wife, b. July 20, 1753, Emma, b. Apr. 16, 1772, Sarah, b. Nov. 12, 1773, Jonathan, b. Oct. 11, '76, Thaddeus, b. Jan. 12, 1779, Nabby, b. Jan. 22, 1782, Sabra, b. Apr. 5, 1784, Elisha, b. June 19, 1786, Emila, b. June 2, 1788, Carissa, b. Dec. 3, 1790, Ruth. b Aug. 4, 1793.

John Lascombe settled in the east part of the town, probably before 1800. He was described as having eccentricities peculiar to himself. Before coming to Hawley, he was a preacher, and very earnest in the cause, but afterward "fell from grace," and used to say that he had preached the everlasting gospel for fifteen years and had told a lie all the time. His children were Francis W. b. Oct 16, 1819, Olive, b. Apr. 8, 1821, Samuel Dorr, b June 27, 1822, resides in Milwaukie, Wis., John Wesley, b. Mar. 8, 1824.

Wm. McIntyre is believed to have settled in the south part of the town in the tract afterward set off to Plainfield, as he appears to have been one of the early residents of that town. He was b. Mar. 1, 1754, Rosannah, his wife, b. Jan. 14, 1756; children, Betsey, b. Dec. 26, 1778, Thomas, b Dec. 22, 1780, William, b. Feb. 2, 1783, Zimri, b. Oct. 2, 1784, Anna, b. Aug. 25, 1786, Major, b. May 3, 1789, Annanias, b. May 1, 1791.

Jonas Rice came from Barre, Mass., about 1785, and settled in the King Corner district. He was b. Oct. 5, 1756, Abigail, his wife, b. Sept. 23, 1764. She was accredited among her neighbors as being possessed of certain powers of witchcraft, and some unaccountable circumstances were supposed to be be attributed to her influence. Their children were Jonas, b. Mar. 22, 1784, Ansel, b. Oct. 26, 1787, Oliver, b. March 21, 1790, m. Desire Taylor, settled in Plainfield, where he d., Orpha, b. Feb. 24, 1796, Jonas 2d, b. July 24, 1798, Abigail, b. June 8, 1800, Sylvanus, b. Mar. 14, 1803, Zeruah, b. Sept. 24, 1805, m. John Braymon, and settled in Ashfield, where she died.

Sylvanus Rice remained on the homestead where his children were born, making two generations reared on the place. He m. Clarissa Carpenter of Savoy. Children, Clarissa J., Rosina, m. Cushman I. Fuller, Elmina, b. Jan. 23, 1832, Julia A., b. Dec. 5, 1833, Newell S., b. Oct. 28, 1836, m. Emeline Starks, and resides in Ohio. He was the first to enlist from Hawley in the War of the Rebellion, going out in the 10th Regt. in the spring of 1861, re-enlisted as a veteran, and served through the entire war. Almon M., b. Dec. 9, 1839. He was possessed of a great desire for romance, went on several whaling voyages, and died on the island of Australia. While there he sent home a box of sea-shells and other curiosities, which was nine months in reaching his parents. Mary F., b. Jan. 13, 1843, m. 1st, Victor A. Bassett, 2d, Daniel Ingraham, and res. in Savoy, Ansel, b. May 4, 1846, d. in infancy, His wife, Clarissa, d. May 7, 1846, and he m. Philinda Bassett of Cummington, d. Aug. 7, 1867. Mr. Rice d. June 9, 1860.

Daniel Rice m. Sarah Brown, and settled near the Savoy line some time about 1800. Children, Lydia, m. Benjamin F. Remington, Stalham, Charlotte, Saphronia, Charlany, b. Sept. 22, 1809, Champion B. b. Sept. 17, 1811, Joanna, b. Sept. 6, 1813, Sarah C. b. Sept. 2, 1815, Daniel, b. April 15, 1818.

Champion B. Rice stayed on the homestead, m. Jane Hollis of Windsor, had Harlan H., drowned Aug. 18, 1858, and Roswell G., a tinner in Conway.

Capt. Luther Rice, brother of Daniel, settled first at Hallockville, having bought of Simeon Crittenden, afterward settled and built where Alonzo F. Turner lives. His children emigrated west at different times, himself and wife afterward joining them there, where they died. Children, Irene, b. Aug. 16, 1816, m. John J. Cook, Luther, b. Jan. 20, 1818, Clarissa, b. March 31, 1820, Calvin, b. Feb. 2, 1823, Loe, b. Sept. 20, 1824, m. Abner Marsh, Sylvester H., b. Jan. 15, 1828, m. Elizabeth J. Smith, Hannah M., b. Sept. 19, 1830, m. Nicholas Dubey.

Moses Rice m. Molly Howes, and they were transient residents. Their children were Rebecca, b. July 13, 1801, m. Rufus Baker, Zelotus, b. March 17, 1803, Moses, b. Dec. 6, 1805, Phebe, b. July 15, 1809, Zelotus 2d, b. June 8, 1811, Marietta, b. Aug. 10, 1813, Roana, b. May 10, 1816, Levi, b Sept. 28, 1818, Abigail, b. April 4, 1821, John W., b. April 29, 1823.

Elias Rice lived in Pudding Hollow; children, Ruth, b. Apr. 14, 1818, Emory, b. Nov. 1, 1820, Sylvester, b Nov. 10, 1822.

Children of Russell and Hannah Hunt; Joseph b. Sept. 22, 1822, Charity, b. July 2, 1825, m. John Taylor, d. in 1855, Hannah, b. June 6, 1828, m. Harvey Hadlock, Ruth, b. Jan. 26, 1830, m. Austin Beals, and lives at North Adams, Betsey, b. June 11, 1833, Russell F. b. June 8, 1834, killed in the war, a few days before his term of enlistment expired, James, b. Aug. 9, 1836, Elisha, b. Oct. 12, 1839, Ebenezer, b. Dec. 23, 1840, Asenath.

Atherton Hunt has always lived where he was born, May 29, 1804, has always been a sound, substantial citizen, and at the age of 83 he is reaping the reward of a life of temperance, sobriety and firm integrity. He m. Betsey Rogers, March 30, 1826. Their children were Moses R., b. Dec. 29, 1826, Henry, b. Aug. 5, 1831, d. in consequence of exposure in the army, and buried in the family lot at Hawley, Martha E., b. Feb. 15, 1834, m. Asa Holden, and resides in Hawley, Josiah H., b. Dec. 26, 1835, m. Laura Richards of Plainfield, is a real estate broker in Topeka, Kansas, Lucius, b. May 26, 1839, remains on the homestead with his father, served in the 52d Regt. is now Town Clerk, Mary E., b. Sept. 22, 1841, lives with her father, John, b. Jan. 18, 1845.

Lucius Hunt m. 1st, Dec. 28, 1868, Sarah E. Holden, and had George W., b. Oct. 4, 1869, Lizzie J., b. Sept. 2, 1871. His wife, Sarah, d. March 21, 1878, and he m. Aug. 19, 1882, Hortense A. Mansfield. Their children are Le Roy T., b. Sept. 7, 1883, Walter F., b. Dec. 28, 1884, Lizzie May, b. May 6, 1886.

Children of Chester Hunt; Adaline, b. Dec. 8, 1821, Mary, b. April 7, 1828, Chester F., b. June 7, 1834, resides in Hawley

John Hunt b. July 4, 1790, m. Feb. 22, 1814, Tryphena Miller, b. Jan 6, 1796. Their children were Josiah, b. Jan. 8, 1815, Jerusha, b. Jan. 27, 1817, Elisha, b. Sept. 22, 1819, Josiah 2d, b. Aug. 7, 1820, James, b. July 8, 1822, William, b. Jan. 27, 1826, James P., b. Sept. 8, 1828, Ann Eliza, b. Aug. 7, 1831, Mary Ann, b. April 1, 1833, John, b. Feb. 27, 1835, Edwin W., b. Oct. 27, 1837, Julia E., b. July 2, 1840, Louise A., b. Feb. 11, 1842.

Elisha Hunt m. Louisa M. Griggs, Aug. 31, 1842, have always lived in Hawley. Their children are Newell, b. Oct. 1, 1843, lives at Diamond Lake, Ill, Lyman G., b. Nov. 15, 1844, lives at Leadville, Col, Ellen J., b. Jan. 15, 1846, m. 1st, Luther Dodge, 2d, Dr. Josiah Trow, and resides in Buckland, Flora L., b. Jan. 30, 1853.

Chester F. Griggs came from Brimfield, was b. Feb. 21, 1794. m. Lydia King, June 13, 1816. Their children were Amos K., b. June 10, 1817, m. Hannah Beals, is a farmer in Plainfield, Lyman F., b. Oct. 19, 1821, m. —— Powers, Clark R., b. March 6, 1824, resides in New York city, Louisa M., b. Feb. 28, 1826, m. Elisha Hunt, and lives in Hawley, Samentha K., b. June 11, 1828, m. Charles A. Brown, and resides at Brimfield, Andrew J., b. July 16, 1830, lives at Chicago, Ill., Charles R., b. Feb. 25, 1836, resides at Westboro.

Noah Cooley was one of the early settlers, and located in the northeast part of the town. The original deed of his land is in possession of his grandson, Calvin E. Cooley, now of Charlemont, and bears the date, July 20, 1771. He was b. in Palmer, Aug. 21, 1741, m. Esther Hyde, b. in Monson, May 31, 1748. Their chileren were Noah, b. March 24, 1781 Esther, b. March 3, 1783, Lovicy, b. Jan. 24, 1785, Asher, b. Jan. 1787, Calvin, b. March 3, 1789, settled in Hawley.

Children of Calvin Cooley; Tryphena, b. Aug 25, 1813, Oramel W., b. Jan. 18, 1816, became a Congregational clergyman, Calvin E., b. June 28, 1822, Pindar F., b. Oct. 14, 1827, resides in Pittsfield.

Calvin E. Cooley remained in Hawley until a few years ago, when he moved to Charlemont. He m. Nov. 1, 1854, Olive F. Crittenden, b. June 6, 1831. Their children were Charles S., b. April 29, 1856, Abbott L., b. Feb 20, 1858, Edwin W., b. June 16, 1859, Olive A., b. Dec. 31, 1861, Clara L., b. Aug. 29, 1863, Abbie R., b. Aug. 15, 1865, Julia C., b. March 2, 1873.

Reuben Cooley was one of the first four families that settled in Hawley in 1771. He was b. June 13, 1746, Margaret, his wife, b. Dec. 15, 1745. Children, Alvin, b. Dec. 9, 1773, Mary, b. Feb. 15, 1775, Sarah, b. May 8, 1777, Orpah, b. March 27, 1781, Reuben Jr., b. Aug. 30, 1783.

Obed Smith, b. April 6, 1770, Rhoda, his wife, b. May, 1771; children, Priscilla, b. Aug. 10, 1794, Obed, b. Nov. 28, 1795.

Joseph Butrick was early identified with the interests of the town and lived east of the present church, afterwards removed to western New York. He was b. Dec. 1, 1773, Polly, his wife, b. Sept. 9, 1776; Children, Susannah, b. Nov. 5, 1797, Moses, b. Nov. 10, 1798, Polly, b. Aug. 20, 1800, Miranda, b. Aug. 8, 1802, Lucinda, b. July 21, 1804, Oliver, b. Aug. 11, 1806, Rosina, b. Oct. 10, 1808, Gracie, b. April 18, 1811, Sarah, b. Feb. 21, 1814.

Children of Elias and Lucinda Goodspeed; Milton, b. Jan. 8, 1801, Sylvia, b. Nov. 4, 1802, Elias, b. Feb. 27, 1805, Nathaniel, b. Dec. 16, 1806, Abigail, b, Aug. 19, 1808, Lucirda, 1. June 24, 1813, Harriet, b. April 9, 1817, Laura, b. Nov. 20, 1820.

Nathaniel Newton was one of the early deacons of the town, his children were Nancy, b. Aug. 29, 1798, became the second wife of Rev. Tyler Thatcher, Julianna, b. Dec. 2, 1800, Hannah, b. Nov. 28, 1803, Phebe Temple, b. Mar. 23, 1807. Sally, b. Oct. 21, 1809.

Children of Joseph and Thankful Howard. William T. b. Oct. 1, 1800, Miranda, b. Aug. 7, 1808, Mercy Jane, b. Oct. 1, 1813.

Asa Blood b. Oct. 20, 1764, Rhoda his wife b. Nov. 26, 1772. Their children were Asa Jr., b. Feb. 24, 1790, Leonard, b. Feb. 16, 1794, Lovain, b. June 15, 1795, Calvin, b. Dec. 19, 1797, Luther, b. Dec. 12, 1799, Electa, b. Dec. 6, 1801.

Abner Blood b. Jan 7, 1766, Rachel his wife b. June 4, 1771. Their children were Prudence, b. May 22, 1788, Betsey, b. Apr. 13, 1793,

Children of Asher and Lydia Cooley; Noah, b. Sept. 1, 1810, Asher, b. April 27, 1812, Sylvanus S. b. Dec. 20, 1813, Lydia C. b. Sept. 14, 1815, Rosamond F. b. Sept. 16, 1817.

Children of Edward and Catharine Baxter; Hannah, b. Oct. 24, 1796, Catharine, b. Dec. 30, 1798, Edward, b. Mar. 17, 1801, Reuben, b. Nov. 5, 1803, Betsey, b. Feb. 8, 1806.

Samuel Russell b. Nov. 15, 1756, Esther his wife b, June 7, 1761. Their children were Zenas, b. Nov. 20, 1785, Eliakim, b. Jan. 10, 1788, Zelotus, b. Sept. 8, 1789, Susanna, b. Sept. 21, 1791.

Spencer Russell b. Nov. 15, 1761, Ruth his wife b. Oct. 15, 1762. Their children were Adnah, b. Dec. 6, 1789, Sylvia, b. Feb. 1792, Allen, b. April 2, 1796.

Children of James and Rebecca Mantor; Nabby W. b. Mar. 2, 1799, Francis, b. June 20, 1803, Moses, b. July 26, 1811, Gratia R. b. Aug. 29, 1814.

Francis Mantor m. Mahala Maynard, July 12, 1832; Their children were Martha W. b. July 28, 1833, Moses M. b. April 23, 1835, resides at Charlemont, is Secretary of the Deerfield Valley Agricultural Society.

Alfred L., b. Sept. 8, 1836, killed in battle at Petersburg, Va., May 6, 1864, Fidelia T. b. Aug. 5, 1838, m. Henry A. Howes, Jan. 1, 1861, resides in Ashfield, Francis W. b. May 28, 1844, enlisted in the 27th Regt. d. of diphtheria at Washington, N. C. Oct. 3, 1862.

Jeremiah Taylor was in early life a sea captain; he came from Yarmouth in 1803, settled near what is known as Fullerville, and raised a large family which have been marked for their ability and influence. Among them were four sons who were prominent clergyman, a notice of which is given elsewhere. Oliver, b. Aug. 18, 1801, Sally, b. Feb. 18, 1804, Martha, b. Sept. 6, 1805, m. Dea. Freeman Hamlin, and lives at Plainfield, Mary, b. Aug. 10, 1807, Timothy, b. Sept. 7, 1809, Rufus, b. March 4, 1811, Mary J., b. Apr. 13, 1813, Mira, b. Apr. 27, 1815, Jeremiah, b. June 1, 1817. The mother of this family was possessed of eminent piety and great strength of character, and although rearing her family in poverty, gave them the example of a christian influence.

Children of Uzziel Simons and Lucy his wife; Rosetta, b. Jan. 28, 1817, Lucy A. b. Aug. 5, 1819, Martin, b. Sept. 10, 1821, Lovina, b. Nov. 18, 1823, Simeon, b. Feb. 11, 1826, Charles, b. Feb. 25, 1828, Hannah b. Feb. 24, 1831, Lydia, b. June 3, 1833, Stephen, b. Feb. 19, 1835, Elvira, b. Feb. 19, 1837.

William Bassett came from Ashfield, was an extensive land owner. His children were Polly, b. Dec. 18, 1818, William O. b. Mar. 30, 1820, resides in Hawley, has been prominent in public affairs, is a large farmer.

Children of Elias and Elizabeth Carrier; Elias, b. Aug. 20, 1816, Louisa, b. Dec. 2, 1819, Joseph H. b. Mar. 18, 1825, resides in Hawley.

Elias Ford was b. in Plainfield, Nov. 25, 1780, m. Sophia Johnson, b. Jan. 6, 1784. They settled on West Hill in 1802 or 3. Their children were Sophia, b. May 18, 1805, m. Noah Ford, Elias, b. July 20, 1807, removed to Albany. N. Y., then to Iowa, where he d., Maria, b. Jan. 14, 1810, m. Isaac Atkins, d. in Conway, July, 23, 1882, Mary, b. May 12, 1812, m. Shubael Bradford, and resides in Conway, William C., b. Nov. 30, 1816, resides in Fairhaven, Sarah C., m. Daniel W. Temple, d. in North Adams, Jane M., b. May 25, 1823, Clynthia T., b. Aug. 14, 1831, m. Wm. B. Martin, and removed west where she died.

Clark Sears was b. in Ashfield, Jan. 30, 1804, m. Emeline Kelly, b. in Ashfield, Jan. 10, 1809, and came to Hawley about 1832. Their children were Clarinda, b. June 30, 1830, m. William Wait and lives in Hawley, Stillman, b. April 6, 1832, d. July 30, 1855, Betsey, b. July 19, 1833, Emeline, b. Feb. 12, 1835, Philena, b. Nov. 20, 1837, m. Alonzo F. Turner, d. Sept. 10, 1857, Hannah, b. June 22, 1839, Ambrose K., b. Nov. 3, 1841, lives in West Hawley, Walter, b. Dec. 23, 1846, lives on the homestead at West Hewley.

Addie Turner b. Aug. 11, 1855, Stillman C. Turner b. July 31, 1857, Frank H. Sears b. Nov. 13, 1868, Foster C. Sears b. June 18, 1886.

Children of Joel and Julia (Baker) Bartlett; Nelly, b. Aug. 9, 1800, Julia, b. Sept. 15, 1802, Joel, b. Aug. 16, 1804, Sally, b. May 4, 1807, m. Robert W. Smith, Laura, b. Mar. 31, 1809, m. Levi Harmon, Fidelia. b. Aug. 2, 1811, m. Edmund Strong, Rhoda, b. Mar. 23, 1818, m. David Strong.

Levi Harmon lived in the old sixth school district, m. Laura Bartlett. Their children were Harriet S. b. Oct. 22, 1833, and lives in Buckland, Ellen J. b. Apr. 4, 1837, m. Jesse M. Ward, and lives in Buckland, Rhoda A. b. Mar. 13, 1839, Charles A., b. June 19, 1841, Fidelia M. b. June 24, 1844, m. Leonard Morse of Royalston, Lewis E., b. June 9, 1849, m. Mrs. Flora G. Crowell.

Gaius Harmon b. Nov. 26, 1799, m. Tempy Vincent, b. Apr. 20, 1802. Children, Paulina W., b. Feb. 23, 1830. Elijah, b. Oct. 7, 1831, Enos, b. Feb. 17, 1833, resides at Hawley, Elijah, b. Nov. 22, 1835, became a Congregational clergyman, resides at Wilmington, Mass., Joseph V., b. Mar. 26, 1837, lives in Florence, Charles T., b. July 10, 1839.

Children of Enos Harmon; Charles F., b. Aug. 7, 1863, d. June 20, 1864, Julia E., b. July 20, 1865, Horace, C., b. April 27, 1869, Nellie P., b. May 2, 1873, Lou M. b. Oct. 24, 1864.

Children of Jonathan and Martha Damon; Moses G., b. July 21, 1828, Cyrus, b. Jan. 9, 1830, Jonathan T., b. March 30, 1832, Stephen W., b. May, 1834, Charles P., b. Sept. 27, 1836, Henry C., b. Nov. 9, 1838, served nine months in the war, is now a farmer in Meriden, Ct., Martha A., b. Dec. 14, 1840, Homer F., b. May 17, 1843, served in the war, now a tinner in New Britain, Ct.

Children of Otis and Roxana Beals; Edmund, b. Dec. 2, 1827, m. Eliza Baker, Roxana, b. Nov. 21, 1830, removed to Ohio, Marila, b. Nov. 28, 1833, Wesley, b. July 22, 1837, lives in Plainfield, Wm. H., b. Aug. 3, 1839, also lives in Plainfield.

John Hadlock, b. Apr. 20, 1772, Mary Ann, his wife, b. June 8, 1777. They came from Williamsburg to Hawley a little before 1800, and settled about half way between Elijah Marsh and Ezra King. He was a carpenter and many buildings are standing that were built by his hands. In April 1834, they removed west where died at advanced ages. They were m. Sept. 13, 1798; Children, Harriet, b. June 18, 1799, m. Horace White. Almira, b. Oct. 9, 1800, m. Dennis Beals, and settled in Plainfield, Velorus, b. Apr. 12, 1802, m. Betsey Pike, and went to Ohio, Hubbard, b. Apr. 9, 1804, m. Lucy Brierly, and removed to California, Lysander, b, Jan. 1, 1806, m. Maria Thompson, Electa, b. Dec. 10, 1807, Lurancy, b. Nov. 7, 1810, m. Gustavus. Dunham, Sibbil, b. July 24, 1812, m. Simeon Harwood, and lives in Hawley, John Jr. b. Sept. 12, 1814, d. 1832, Harvey, b. Nov. 12, 1822, m. Hannah Hunt, d. April 2, 1867. The children of this family were possessed of a very natural ability for music, both vocal and instrumental, but circumstances seemed to prevent their making much capital from that ability. Their descendants of the second and third generation inherit the same gift.

Rufus Sprague m. Emma Loomis, and lives in the old sixth district near the Moody spring. Children, Clark F. b. Aug. 7, 1832, d. March 25, 1863, from the war, Maria A. b. Oct. 18, 1835, Susan b. Feb. 27, '38, m. Wilson Gould, Asher B., b. Apr. 27, 1840, has a war record, lives in Hawley, Emma A., b. July 7, 1842, Laura E. b. Aug. 15, 1845, John F. b. 1850, m. — Roberts.

Chester Upton lived a term of years near where William Wait now lives, afterward removed to Haydenville. He m. Mirmelia Edgarton, April 3, 1828; children, Asa W., b. Feb. 18, 1833, Aurelia, b. Feb. 14, 1835, Mary Ann, b. Sept. 4, 1837, Lucy B., b. Nov. 13, 1840, Sarah M., b. Oct. 16, 1844.

Col. Noah Joy was b. in Plainfield, Feb. 27, 1782, m. Jan. 21, 1806, Persis Warner, b. in Hardwick, Aug. 17, 1783. They came to Hawley soon after their marriage and settled in the south part of the town, where he built and run a hotel, known as "Joy's Tavern," until his death, May 23, 1843, and was the South Hawley postmaster. Their children were Laura, b. Oct. 29, 1806, m. Samuel T. Grout, d. Aug. 31, 1861, Annis, b. Oct. 8, 1808, m. Levi Holden Jr., d. Jan. 17, 1857, Eliza, b. Dec. 11, 1810, m. Calvin S. Longley, Hannah, b. Sept. 15, 1812, m. Ashbel W. Carter, Merrick, b. Dec. 27, 1814, d. June 12, 1840, Lorenzo W., b. Dec 15, 1817, resides at Northampton, where he was for a long time the postmaster, and like many others was removed to gratify President Cleveland's partisan spirit, Nelson, b. Jan. 17, 1820, m. Mabaleth King, lives at Shelburne Falls, Henry C., b. Aug. 5, 1823, m. Jerusha King, resides at Shelburne Falls, Mariette, b. April 5, 1830.

Children of Levi and Sally Eldridge; Mary P. b. Apr. 29, 1814, Sally, b. Mar. 18, 1817, Levi. b. Nov. 3, 1818, Roswell, b. May 26, 1821, Sally M. b. Nov, 6, 1822, Laura A. b. Aug. 2. 1824, Lemuel, b. Nov. 22, '26, Adaline C. b. Aug. 24, 1828, Thomas L. b. Oct. 29, 1830, Charles G., b. Aug. 14, 1833, Charlotte A. b. Sept. 5, 1835, Malesta E. b. May 2, 1839.

Millo T. Carter lived where Lewis J. Hall now lives. Children, Thomas M. b. July 17, 1832, m. Flora A. Vincent, resides in Williamsburg, Phineas S. b. July 4, 1834, has owned a sheep ranch in Kansas, Ellen R. b. Nov. 25, 1836, m. A. L. Avery, and resides in Charlemont, Sylvia C. b. Oct. 17, 1838,. m. Thomas Mayhew, resides at Shelburne Falls, Maria, b. Sept. 25, 1848, m. Kendrick T. Slate, resides in Greenfield.

Sanderson E. Carter m. Tirzah Stiles and had one daughter, Delia, m. Isaac C. Vincent, and lives at West Hawley.

Ashbel W. Carter m. Hannah Joy, and now lives at Shelburne Falls. Children, Noah Joy, — Olive W. b. Jan. 29, 1836, Washburn H. b. Dec. 3, 1837, Edwin T. b. Apr. 15, 1846.

Henry B. White m. Nancy Gibbs of Otis. Their children are Nellie U., b. Dec. 30, 1861, m. Frank E. Mason, Melvin H., b. Mar. 12, 1863, Nora E., b. Dec. 30, 1864, Myrtle L., b. Oct. 30, 1866, Inez S., b. Nov. 23, 1868, Charles F., b. May 29, 1870, Julia E., b. April 13, 1872, Mabel E., b. Jan. 21, 1878, Maud I., b. March 15, 1882.

Children of Clesson and Mary Smith; They lived a little west of the old meeting house, and several of the children were deaf and dumb. Mary H., b. Aug. 31, 1803, Samuel S., b. Jan. 8, 1805, Elihu, b. May 9, 1806, Moses M., b. Sept. 28, 1807, Consider, b. Oct. 21, 1808, Wm., b. Jan. 10, 1810, Samuel S., b. Feb. 4, 1813, Minerva, b. Mar. 19, 1815, Anna, b. Jan. 4, 1820, Simeon, b. June 25, 1826.

Rufus Hall m. Keziah Hall, Nov. 29, 1810. They lived in Pudding Hollow, where William Thayer now lives, afterwards went to Williamsburg. Children. Sylvia, b. Jan. 29, 1812, Mary, b. Aug. 23, 1813, Sylvester, b. May 29, 1820, Keziah E, b. July 1, 1823, Philena H., b. Aug. 30, 1825.

Children of Elder John and Catharine Breed; Charles W., b. Sept. 21, 1822, Catharine. b. June 3, 1826, Henry G., b. Jan. 11, 1828, Martha A., b. May 18, 1831.

Dr. Daniel Fobes was an early physician of the town, and had Daniel L. B., b. March 12, 1797, Olive H., b. April 26, 1801.

Ebenezer Healy came from Chesterfield and lived east of Geo. Starks' sawmill, where Rowland Sears now lives. Children, Elizabeth, b. Sept. 27, 1815, Mary, b. June 6, 1818, m. Horace Thayer, Caroline, b. Feb. 26, 1820, Lucretia, b. Oct. 17, 1824, m. David Hastings, Jonathan E., b. April 21, 1827, Harriet, b. Dec. 23, 1831, Wealthy,—

Ebenezer Crowell came early and settled in Pudding Hollow. He was b. Jan. 29, 1736, Phebe his wife b. Aug. 17, 1757. Children, Rebecca, b. Mar. 2, 1781, m. Hollister Baker, Phebe. b. Jan. 22, 1782, Erede, b. May 9, 1784, Elizabeth, m. Warriner King, b. Sept. 21, 1788, Ebenezer, b. Aug. 5, 1792, Edward, b. Aug. 16, 1794, Allen, b. Nov. 8, 1798.

Children of Edward and Apphia Crowell; Elisha, b. Mar. 12, 1821, Elizabeth V., b. June 16, 1823, m. Edwin Warriner, Mary, b. May 16, 1825, m. Wm. R. Thayer, Rebecca b. May 31, 1827, Edward L., b. Aug. 19, 1829, m. Flora G. Dickinson, and settled in Hawley, Rebecca 2d b. Feb. 15, 1832, Harriet, b. July 31, 1839.

Children of Ebenezer and Hannah Crowell; David, b. Sept. 14, 1813, Lovina b. Sept. 14, 1814, Phebe Bangs, b. Mar. 12, 1816, Luther F. b. June 31, 1818, Hannah, b. Aug. 4, 1820.

Ebenezer Thayer was a stirring business man, and lived in several places in town, afterward went to Charlemont, where he kept the hotel. He m. Phebe Crowell, their children were Zilpha, b. Jan.

22, 1804, Hollister Baker, b. Oct. 31, 1805, Phebe, b. Apr. 6, 1808, Ebenezer, b. June 14, 1810, Elizabeth, b. Sept. 12, 1812, John, b. Oct. 9, 1814, is a wealthy farmer in Greenfield, Wm. R. lives in Hawley.

Silas Dodge was an early settler in the east part of the town. His children were Thomas, b. April 6, 1793, Esther, b. March 9, 1795, Mason, b. Dec. 30, 1797, Hiram, b. April 6, 1799, settled in Hawley, Silvina, b. May 31, 1801, Eunice, b. Aug. 7, 1803, Silas, b. Aug. 2, 1805, m. Adaline Carrier, settled in Hawley, d. Oct. 9, 1886, Luther, b. Sept. 28, 1807, Elmina, b. Feb. 28, 1810, Eber, b. April 21, 1812, Content, b. Nov. 8, 1814, Fanny, b. June 19, 1818, Charles, b. Oct. 19, 1820, a lawyer in Toledo, Ohio.

Children of Silas and Adaline Dodge; Palixana, b. March 17, 1834, m. Wm. O. Bassett, Elizabeth, b. Nov. 19, 1835, Luther, b. June 11, 1840, m. Ellen J. Hunt, lived and d. in Hawley.

Children of Hiram Dodge; Alonzo T., b. Dec. 5, 1833, Clinton H., b. Nov. 15, 1835, resides in Hawley, was in the 52d Regt., was in the Legislature of 1879, has been Selectman &c., Euphelia B., b. Dec. 7, 1837, Lucy, b. March 26, 1840, Mason W., b. March 29, 1843, Roana M., b. Nov. 29, 1845, Tyler H., b. May 6, 1852.

Noah Ford and Sophia Ford were m. Apr. 21, 1831, and lived a few years on West Hill. Their first three children were b. in Hawley as follows; John Wesley, b. Jan. 21, 1832, m. Calista Ford of Lenox, and resides at Stockbridge, Hester A., b. Apr. 19, 1833, m. Francis F. Briggs and lives in Windsor, Elisha W., b. Apr. 17, 1836, lives in Kan.

Elijah Ford. b. Dec. 8, 1759, Anna, his wife b. June 21, 1759. Children, Melinda, b. July 16, 1787, Flijah, b. May 23, 1789. Polly, b. June 3, 1791, Mary, b. July 11, 1793, Anna, b. July 28, 1796.

Children of Jonathan and Charlotte Wells; Emma, b. Feb. 6, 1809, Charlotte, b. Mar. 16, 1813, Judith B., b. Aug. 14, 1814, Willard, b. Aug. 8, 1816, Wealthy, b. Dec. 6, 1818, Sally, b. Sept. 2, 1820.

Children of Joseph and Betsey Barnard; Prudence, b. April 10, 1803, Almira, b. July 15, 1804, Diana, b. June 3, 1806, Daniel W., b. Jan. 21, 1808, Joseph, b. Jan. 15, 1811.

Children of William and Rhoda Sprague; Lovina, b. Sept. 26, 1808, m. Anthony Sears, and settled in Hawley, Wm., b. Sept. 20. 1809, Eli, b. Sept. 6, 1810, Rhoda, b. Sept. 5, 1811, Rosamond, b. Sept. 29, 1812.

The Crosbys, once numerous, now extinct in town, settled in different parts of the town, particularly in Pudding Hollow and the old sixth district. Their representatives are abroad to a considerable extent. Theophilus Crosby b. Mar. 29, 1779, Phebe, his wife b. Mar 6, 1786. Children; Daniel, b. Apr. 4, 1806, Theophilus, b. July 12, 1812, Judah, b. Dec. 26, 1814, Sally W., b. Oct. 16, 1817, Phebe H., b. June 5, 1820, Samuel C., b. Oct. 16, 1822.

Judah Crosby b. June 10, 1777, Charlotte, his wife, b. July 10, 1785. Children, David T., b. Jan. 15, 1808, Judah, b. March 12, 1810, Chillingsworth, b. July 26, 1812.

Eben Crosby settled in Pudding Hollow. His children were Daniel, b. June 13, 1812. settled in Hawley, Sarah, b. April 20, 1814, Joshua, b. Oct. 21, 1816, Hannah, Oct. 23, 1818, Reuben, b. Sept. 6, 1820.

Children of Asher and Abigail Loomis; Noah, b. Feb. 16, 1803, Emma W., b. Jan. 4, 1807, Francis, b. Nov. 22, 1809, Freburn, b. Aug. 27, 1811, Abigail, b. Aug. 25, 1816, Parthena, b. July 29, 1820, Pembroke, b. April 15, 1824.

Asa Vining came from Weymouth in June, 1806. His children were David, Martin and Sally, the two last never married.

Children of David and Gratia Vining; David T., b. Oct. 19, 1821, a physician in Conway, Gratia, b. June 25, 1824, Thomas, b. Feb. 14, '26, Mary, b. March 14, 1828, Edwin, b. Feb. 14, 1830.

James Doane b. in Hadley, May 13, 1768, d. May 28, 1838, Lucy Woodbridge b. Jan. 6, 1765, d. Dec. 29, 1835. They were m. Sept. 27, 1790, and settled east of the old church. Children, Allen, b. Dec. 18, 1791, d. Jan. 23, 1835, Patty R., b. July 4, 1793. d. May 28, 1874, Louisa, b. Jan. 3, 1799, d. Dec 11, 1855, Lucy, b. Aug. 14, 1800. m. Bardine Damon, and settled in Hawley, d. Dec. 7, 1869, William, b. April 20, 1802, d. Oct. 16, 1826, Mary W., b. Mar. 3, 1804, d. in infancy, James Jr., b. Mar. 2, 1806, settled in Hawley, d. Jan. 20, 1872.

James Doane Jr., m. Cordelia B. Sanford, b. Jan. 12, 1811, d. Dec. 1, 1880. Their children were Martha A., b. June 20, 1832, m. Geo. Jourdian in Ohio, in 1859, now resides at Northampton, James Wm., b. Sept. 26, 1833, was a member of the 52d Regt., and has filled several town offices, Helen C., b. Jan. 10, 1838, m. Franklin Beals, resides in Florence, Sylvia, E., b. Dec. 27, 1844, m. James Eggleston, George W., b. May 4, 1848, m. Julia Williams, resides in Holyoke.

J. William Doane lives on the old Dr. Moses Smith place, next east of his birthplace. He m. Angeline Butler of Buckland, May 29, 1864. Their children are Frank B., b. Sept. 12, 1865, now in Amherst College, Carrie Ida, b. May 26, 1867, Sarah Delia. b. June 1, 1869, Fred W., b. Feb. 11, 1871, Willie N., b. Aug. 27. 1872.

William Sanford came from Saybrook. Ct., m. 1st, Betsey Parker, had William, Betsey, b. 1800, m. Cushing Shaw, d. in 1884; he m. 2d, Nubby Hawks, and had Cordelia B., b. Jan. 12, 1811, m. James Doane, and another dau. m. Augustus Belding of Pittsfield.

William Sanford Jr. m. Rebecca Damon, and had three children, two sons, William and Dwight, now living in Hartford, Ct.

Children of Bardin and Rebecca Damon; Electa, b. Dec. 21, 1818, Phiddia, b. June 12, 1821, Allen D., b. Dec. 4, 1835.

Oliver Shattuck b. July 29, 1750, Lucy, his wife, b. Jan. 19, 1751, Children, Oliver, b. May 11, 1778, Amelia, b. Dec. 30, 1779, Sally, b. Sept. 19, 1781, Justice, b. March 1, 1783, Henry and Harriet, twins, b. May 15, 1786, Calvin, b. July 30, 1790, Thera, b. Aug. 1, 1792.

John Taylor is believed to have been the first Taylor that settled in Hawley, although one account gives the name as Adonijah. (It is probable that this name, as it appears on page 37, in the chapter on the early settlement, is not correct.) John Taylor settled just above Pudding Hollow in 1771, being one of the first four families in town. He was b. Nov. 30, 1752, Elizabeth, his wife, b. Sept. 22, 1748. Their children were John Jr., b. Sept. 9, 1781, Dolly, b. Sept. 2, 1783, Rachel, b. Sept. 29, 1785, Shays, b. March 7, 1787.

John Taylor Jr., settled in Hawley and m. Loney Barnard. Children, Henry, b. Sept. 9, 1803, resides in Williamsburg, Edward, b. Sept. 4, 1805, Loney, b. June 24, 1807, m. Reuben Crittenden and settled in Hawley, Adonijah, b. Nov. 10, 1810, Daniel, b. Oct. 12, 1812. m. Jane Farrar and settled in Cummington, Shays, b. Jan. 5, 1815, Elizabeth, b. May 17, 1817, John, b. Oct. 18, 1823, m. Charity Hunt, lives in Savoy, Hannah, m. Ira Joy.

Nathan West lived in Bozrah for a term of years, and removed to "Gallows Hill" in Northampton. He was b. Sept. 18, 1746, Sarah, his wife, b. Jan. 1, 1747. Children, Asa, b, Nov. 30, 1770, Bille, b. June 13, 1772, Nathan Jr., b. Oct. 21, 1773, John, b. May 21, 1787.

Children of Salmon and Anna Graves; Roxana, b. Apr. 1818, Daniel, b. May 6, 1820, Rhoda, b. July 2, 1822, Jerusha, b. Apr. 1, 1824.

John Starks was b. in Lyme, N. H., Nov. 30, 1783, d. May 2, 1867. Anne Rogers was b. In Conway, April 3, 1785, d. Feb. 3, 1868. They were m. Sept. 17, 1807, and settled in the southwest part of Hawley about the time of their marriage, where they passed the rest of their lives, covering a period of sixty years. Their children were Phineas, b. June 5, 1809, Rufus, b. Mar. 21, 1812, settled in Savoy, was an Advent preacher, d. May 2, 1885, Daniel, b. Oct. 18, 1816, and went to Ohio in early life, where he has since resided, Laura A., b. April 21, 1822, m. Thomas K. Wheeler and lives in Plainfield.

Phineas Starks remained on the homestead, and m. Feb. 20, 1834, Almira King of Chesterfield, b. May 27, 1817. Their children were Mary Ellen, b. Aug. 18, 1839, m. Wm. H. Deming, d. ——, Henry Watson, b. April 14, 1842, m. Emma M. Temple, Sept. 4, 1862, resides at North Adams, Fanny L., b. Dec. 14, 1844, m. Amos D. Taylor, Nov. 10, 1864, and lives at the homestead, George K, b. April 10, 1851, m. Nettie A. Hubbard, and resides in Hawley.

Children of Dennis and Fanny (Starks) Taylor. Frank W., b. July 2, 1868, Bertie, b. Feb. 11, '72, d. Apr. 15 1873, Hattie, b. Aug. 17, '74.

Three generations have been born and reared on this farm, making four successive generations living there. This furnishes an evidence that farming on the old hills of New England may be made a success.

Henry W. Starks has one daughter Cora, b. in Hawley, May 20, 1865.

Samuel Wheeler m. Hannah King, Mar. 28, 1811, and settled near Hallockville, at the birthplace of Jonas King, the missionary, who was a brother of Mrs. Wheeler. Their children were Thomas K., b. March 29, 1812, m. Laura Starks, lives in Plainfield, Daniel D., b. Oct. 10, '13, m. — Plunkett of Adams, and was for a long time associated with his father-in-law in a manuf'g business under the company name of Plunkett & Wheeler, Jonas K., b. Oct. 26, 1815, removed west in early life.

Giles Atkins, b. in Middletown, Ct., moved to Whately, m. Martha Graves, had Elisha, b. Dec. 1795. His wife d. and he m. Sally Crittenden, lived a few years in Coleraine, and moved in 1807 to Plainfield, on the Hawley line, a part of the farm being in Hawley. The family attended school in Hawley and in various ways were identified with the interests of the town. His second wife d. and he m. Ruth Fairbanks, who survived him, and d. in Hawley, June 23, 1861. Two of his sons by his second mariage settled in Hawley, as follows:—

Freeman Atkins was b. in Coleraine, Aug. 21, 1806, m. Rebecca Baker of Hawley, Dec. 11, 1827, d. Nov. 30, 1879. Their children were Louisa, b. April 26, 1828, m. Benjamin Sears, settled in Hawley, d. Feb. 14, 1868, Harriet, b. Jan. 28, 1832, d. Nov. 21, 1835, Almon, b. July 31, 1836, d. at No. Hadley. Nov. 11, 1861, Francis W., b. Sept. 19, 1840.

Francis W. Atkins m. Lovisa Blanchard, May 15, 1867, succeeds his parents on the homestead, it being the Zenas Bangs place, has two children, Carrie L., b. Oct 4, 1869, Carlos A., b. Oct. 2, 1876.

Isaac Atkins was b. in Coleraine, July 16, 1808, m. Nov. 16, 1829, Maria Ford of Hawley, b. Jan. 14, 1810, d. July 22, 1882. He d Mar. 4, 1884. Their children were William G., b. Oct. 1, 1836, m. Julia M. White of Cummington, Oct. 1, 1862, James Laroy, b. May 10, 1841, m. Anna M. Vining, resides in Conway. has a son, Isaac Deloss.

William G. Atkins resides in Cummington, has one son, Almon W., b. May 23, 1864.

Aaron Gould was an old resident in the old sixth district. He was b. March 14, 1806, d. Dec. 17, 1886, Lucinda, his wife b. Aug. 5, 1806. Their children were Lemuel, b. May 6, 1833, Wilson, b. Oct. 31, 1835, Daniel H., b. Nov. 23, 1839, lives in Plainfield, Gilbert A., b. July 23, 1842, Joanna R., b. Sept. 26. 1844, Mary Ann, b. Jan. 13, 1847, Luther E., b. Feb. 4, 1851.

Children of Lemuel Gould; Albert L., b. Nov. 9, 1863, Willie S., b. May 24, 1865, George W., b. April 20, 1867, Charles H., b. Nov. 19, 1868, Atta B., b. June 9, 1871, Herbert L., b. March 12, 1873.

Wilson Gould m. Susan Sprague, June 4, 1857. Their children were Clarence W., b. June 7, 1860, Erwin F., b. Dec. 12, 1864, Laura E., b. July 18, 1871. His wife, Susan d. July 18, 1877, and he m. Julia K. Mitchell, Dec. 28, 1878.

Children of Daniel H. Gould; Carrie E., b. April 17, 1862, Clark F., b. Feb. 19, 1863.

Children of Gilbert A. Gould; Flora A., b. Sept 5, 1864, Frank L., b. Oct. 3, 1866, Rosie E., b. Nov. 6, 1868, James A., b. July 20, 1870, James W., b. May 8, 1880, Merritt C., b. Oct. 18, 1883.

Children of Luther E. Gould; Viola E., b. April 3, 1876, Gracie, b. Oct. 20, 1882.

Alpheus Hawkes was b. Dec. 26, 1786, d. Mar. 18, 1859. Polly Washburn b. June 19, 1788, d. Mar. 8, 1848. They were m. June 9, 1808. Their children were Roana N., b. May 7, 1809, d. Feb. 18, 1832, William b. Sept 26, 1810, John W., b, March 28, 1813, m. Harriet Baker, Fanny M., b. Jan. 3, 1816, Adaline, b. July 6, 1817, d. Jan 20, 1839, James R. b. Jan. 21, 1819, d. Dec. 3, 1861, Benjamin W., b. June 16, 1820, Experience H., b. Oct. 16, 1821, Levi, b. Jan. 5, 1824, Margaret, b. April 4, 1826, Olive, b. March 20, 1828, Alpheus Jr., b June 1, 1830

Levi Hawkes settled in Hawley and m. Ann Fuller, b. Aug. 23, 1831. Their children were Clara A., b. Nov. 30, 1850, William H., b. July 24, 1852, m. Mrs. Martha J. Stiles, and lives in Hawley, Lucius, b. Mar. 6, 1856, Julia A., b. Jan. 14, 1858, m. 1st, Wallace Cleveland. 2d, ——, and resides in Northampton, James R., b. June 21, 1860, resides in Boston. His wife, Ann, d. and he m. 2d, Mrs. Bathsheba Ayres. By this marriage his children are Charles D., b. March 1, 1865, lives at Northampton, Albert E., b. Feb. 28, 1871.

Children of Ichabod and Perliua Hawkes. Dwight W., b. Nov. 27, 1812, Lucius, b. Nov. 7, 1814, Henry, b. April 2, 1817, Juliette, b. Oct. 2, 1819, Henry, b. Jan. 17, 1822, Charles, b. Feb. 2, 1824, Catharine, b. Sept. 2, 1827, Hiram, b. Aug. 13, 1829, Samuel, b. April 9. 1832.

Zadock Hawkes, b. Sept. 15, 1770, Rhoda, his wife, b. Jan. 1, 1775; Children, Amelia, b. Nov. 22, 1798, Levi, b. April 7, 1800, Olive and Issa, twins, b. June 4, 1802. a daughter b. and d. May 7, 1804, Zadock b. Aug. 8, 1805, Consider, b. Oct. 16, 1807, Jeremiah L., b. Apr. 8, 1811.

Asher Hawkes, b. Oct. 13, 1764, Micah, his wife, b. March 24, 1770. Children, Sarah, b. Aug. 20, 17— Simeon, b. Sept. 18, 1790, Caroline, b. Feb. 4, 1793.

Children of Edward and Ruth Darby. Levi, b. Nov. 15, 1794, Ebenezer, b. Nov. 20, 1798, Freeman. b. Oct. 3, 1801, Olive, b. Aug. 9, 1803, Gracie, b. Nov. 3, 1805, Lyman, b. July 2, 1807, Roswell, b. Nov. 17, 1809, Erastus, b. Sept. 14, 1810.

Oliver Patch b. Nov. 30, 1778, Polly, his wife, b. Sept.19, 1781. Children, Lucy L., b. Sept. 3, 1805, Henry, b. Nov. 1, 1806, Fidelia, b. Feb. 14, 1808, Electa, b. July 23, 1810, Oliver, b. July 3, 1815.

Children of Erastus and Sarah Mansfield; Sarah, b. 1827, B. Parsons, b. 1828, resides in Easthampton, Christopher L., b. Dec. 1, 1829, Susanna A., b. Sept. 9, 1831, Wesson E., b. Jan. 20, 1834, and resides in Hawley.

Children of Ozias and Hannah Davis; Daniel A., b. Nov. 11, 1828, Frederick S., b. Jan. 31, 1830.

Zebedee Wood came from Bozrah, Conn., and settled in Bozrah. It is evident by records left by him that he came to Hawley in 1774. He was a tanner and shoemaker before and after his removal, and was identified with the public interests of his day. He was b. March 20, 1732, Esther, his wife, b. July 29, 1736. Children, Sibel, b. July 29, 1765, Ruth, b. March 11, 1767, Ann, b. Sept. 8. 1771, Thomas, b. Dec. 11, 1772, became a congregational clergyman, Esther, b. June 30, 1776. It has been said that Esther was the first female child born in Hawley, but we are not aware of the facts of the case. She m. Zimri Longley, and lived to an advanced age.

Children of Andrew and Anna Wood; Betsey b. Aug. 9, 1792, John H., b. Feb. 15, 1795, settled in Hawley, Fitch, b. Sept. 4, 1796, settled in Hawley, Sarah, b. June 4, 1798, David, b. March 12, 1800, Jonathan, C., b. Feb. 7, 1804, Zebedee, b. Sept. 16, 1805.

Fitch Wood m. Mrs. Peggy Hall, Jan. 1, 1826. Children, Ebenezer H., b. Oct. 25, 1826, Martha A., b. Oct. 9, 1828, Andrew and Thomas, twins, b. April 24, 1831, Margaret, b. May 26. 1833, Arabel, b. April 16, 1836.

Simeon Crittenden came from Rehoboth, settled at Hallockville at an early date. He was b. Jan. 28, 1762, Lucretia, his wife, b. Jan. 21, 1767, Children, David, b. Sept. 2, 1791, a very active business man, once owned the gristmill in Charlemont, Persis, b. Nov. 7, 1790, Simeon, b. May 7, 1796, Lucretia, b. Oct. 8, 1797.

Simeon Crittenden, son of Simeon. settled in Hawley, in the part known as Bozrah. He m. Esther Lathrop, Dec. 21,1826. Children, George D., b. Aug. 30, 1827, m. — Dawes, and resides in Shelburne Falls, Lucretia, b. Sept. 20, 1829, Olive, b. June 6, 1831, m. Calvin E. Cooley, resides at Charlemont, Caroline H., b. Feb. 21, 1833, Rebecca, b. March 5, 1835, lives on the homestead, Charles, b. Jan. 1, 1837, lives on the homestead.

Theodore Field lived in the northeast part of the town. His children were Thomas, b. Aug. 5, 1815, Theodore, b. Dec. 7, 1816, Samuel T., b. April 20, 1820, Deborah, b. Sept. 9, 1818, Caroline, b. Oct. 31, 1822, Rosamond, b. Oct. 22, 1824, Elijah, b. May 22, 1828, Edmund, b. July, 1831.

Children of Samuel and Jemima Dickinson; Albert F., b. June 28, 1809, Justice M., b. Apr. 23, 1811, Mary Ann, b. Sept 21, 1812, Abigail b. Feb. 23. 1815, Harriet and Samuel, twins, b. July 19, 1817, John, b. May 3, 1821.

Children of Ebenezer and Tryphena Dickinson; Roswell, b. Sept. 18, 1816, Abner, b. Oct. 15, 1819, Harriet, b. May 15, 1821.

Children of Harvey and Lydia Strong; Amasa, b. Feb. 27, 1814, Lewis, b. April 12, 1817, Jonas, b. Sept. 8, 1819.

Children of William and Gratia Patch; Gratia M., b. Apr. 27, 1810, William, b. Dec. 9, 1811, Eli H., b. Dec 25, 1812, Angeline S., b. May 24, 1814, Mary Ann, b. Oct. 4, 1816, Luther, b. June 6, 1818, Alathea, b. Aug. 20, 1819, a daughter b. Jan. 24, 1821, Jonas K., b. June 12, 1824.

Children of Sylvester and Lovina Porter; Edward H., b. Sept. 27, 18-33, Simeon D., b. June 17, 1838, Mary L., b. July 28, 1841, George, H., b. Oct. 2, 1844.

Children of Ebenezer and Eunice Porter; Sarah J., b. Mar. 12, 1825, Mehitable F., b. Nov. 26, 1826, Abigail, b. Aug. 31, 1828.

Children of Moses and Mehitable Rogers; Almira, b. Mar. 11, 1801, Ahira, b. June 14, 1803, Elias, b. Aug. 9, 1805, Polly, b. Sept. 24, 1807. Dr. Charles L. Knowlton was b. May 3, 1824.

Children of Stephen and Orpha Pixley; Orrilla, b. Oct. 21, 1805, Alvan C., b. Oct. 19, 1809, Lorenzo, b. March 10, 1812, Stephen, b. Apr. 1, 1831, Sumner, b. Feb. 3, 1816.

Hezekiah Warriner settled in the east part of the town at an early date, was influential and prominent in town affairs. His son Hezekiah Jr., settled in Hawley and m. Hannah Porter, May 29, 1817. Children, Justin Bliss, b. Mar. 15, 1818, Edwin, b. May 10, 1819, m. Elizabeth Crowell, lived and d. in Hawley, Benjamin Leonard, b. Sept. 15, 1820, Hezekiah Ryland, b. July 23, 1822, Henry Augustus, b. Sept. 21, 1824.

Alvah Page lived in the northeast part of the town. His children were Alvah, b. Mar. 17, 1806, became a congregational clergyman, Clarinda, b. Dec. 19, 1807, Charles Austin, b. Sept. 21, 1809, Horatio Franklin, b. Sept. 21, 1811, became a physician, Theophilus, b. July 9, 1813. Rebecca, b. Sept. 17, 1815, Irwin B., Jan. 16, 1818, Phineus Loyd, b. July 20, 1819, became a lawyer and resides at Ann Arbor, Mich., Joel Stanley b., April 26, 1822, became a lawyer, Baalis B., b., Mar. 24, 1824, Lynthia A., b. Sept. 30, 1829.

Zephaniah Lathrop was b. March 9, 1760, Rachel, his wife, b. Feb. 1764. Children, Sibel, b. Feb. 21, 1785, Arabella, b. Sept. 25, 1786, Daniel, b. Aug. 8, 1788, Samuel, b. Aug. 17, 1790, Zephaniah Jr. b. Dec. 23, 1792, George, b. March 5, 1795, settled in Hawley, Thomas, b. Jan. 7, 1797. Esther, b. Jan. 8, 1799, m. Simeon Crittenden, Myron, b. June 30, 1801, Jedediah, b. Feb. 15, 1804, Edwin, b. Aug. 2, 1807, Ephraim, b. Jan. 8, 1811.

Children of Zephaniah Jr. and Tryphena Lathrop; Henry W., b. Oct. 20, 1819, Rachel W., b. Jan 21. 1821.

Children of Zerah and Clarissa Graham; Abigail T., b. Jan. 7, 1818, Eliza, b. April 30, 1820, Hart T., b. May 27, 1821, Proctor M., b. Sept. 22, '22, John Q. A., b. Dec. 25, ' 28.

Children of Erastus and Naomi Hitchcock; Whitney J., b. Dec. 24, 1813, Dwight W., b. Feb. 29, 1816, Eliza H., b. Nov. 3, 1817, Erastus P., b. Jan. 28, 1820, Samuel J., b. June 28, 1822, Emily N., b. July 8, 1824, Albert, b. June 8, 1827, Olive, b. June 11, 1829.

Children of Samuel Jr. and Tirzah Hitchcock; Sylvia B., b. Jan. 30, 1799, Simeon C., b. July 1, 1801, Wealthy, b. Nov. 6, 1805.

Children of Simeon and Almina Hitchcock; Maria T., b. Jan. 4, 1825, Almina E., b. Feb. 22, 1827, Marion, b. Sept. 13, 1828, Hannah E., b. April 20, 1831, Arthur, b. June 29, 1833, Catharine C., b. Oct. 1841.

Children of Eli and Ann B. Hitchcock; Horatio W., b. Jan. 21, 1817, Catharine K., b. July 18, 1818, Ann J., b, Sept. 11, 1820, Eli N., b. July 21, 1823, Lyman A., b. March 18, 1827.

David Parker b. Oct. 15, 1747, Sarah, his wife, b. July 25, 1750. Children. Sally, b. April 25, 1773, Rhoda, b. Jan. 1, 1775, David, b. May 8, 1777, Levi, b. July 31, 1779, Edmund, b. July 11, 1785, Eleanor b. July 15, 1787, Oreb, b. Nov. 22, 1789, Consider, b. Oct. 31, 1792.

Children of Rhoda and Abel Parker; Clarissa, b. April 7, 1819, Rhoda, b. April 9, 1822, a son, b. Nov. 20, 1832.

Olive Hall b. July 1, 1776, Seth Hall b. Aug. 22, 1783, Phebe Hall b. March 6, 1786, Rufus Hall b. Aug. 26, 1788, Persis Hall b. June 26, '91.

Children of Seth and Erede Hall; Erede C., b. Feb. 10, 1806, Roana, b. June 7, 1810, Harrison, b. Nov. 21, 1812, Seth, b. July 10, 1815, Allen R., b. Oct. 13, 1817.

Children of John and Sybil Tobey; Joshua W., b. Jan. 31, 1821, Samuel, b. Nov. 8, 1822, John W. b. Aug. 3, 1828.

MARRIAGES.

1795 May 7, William Parker and Mehitable Lilly.
" Dec. 24, Rufus Baker and Olive Hall.
1797 Dec. 13, Joseph Longley and Mrs. Lucy Shattuck.
" Sept. 19, William Sanford and Betsey Parker.
1798 Dec. 8, Sylvanus Marsh and Martha Parker.
1799 Oct. 22, Hollister Baker and Rebecca Crowell.
1800 Jan. 9, Levi Holden and Mary Longley.
" Feb. 28, Alvan Sears and Bethiah Howes.
" Feb. Moses Rice and Molly Howes.

1801 Nov. 19, Alden Sears and Sarah Crosby.
1802 Nov. 1, John Taylor and Loney Barnard.
1804 Feb. 6, Theophilus Crosby and Phebe Hall.
1805 Oct. 26, Edmund Longley and Olive Field.
1806 Sept. 21, Ezra King and Jerusha King.
" Oct. 23, Zenas Bangs and Nabby Crosby.
1807 Rev. Thomas Wood and Olive Longley.
1808 Luther Longley and Harriet Shattuck.
1809 Nov. 29, Uzziel Simons and Lucy Coney.
1810 March 15, William Sanford and Abigail Hawkes.
" March 24, Dr. Moses Smith and Mrs. Ann Fobes.
" Nov. 29, Rufus Hall and Keziah Hall.
1811 March 28, Samuel Wheeler and Hannah King.
" Oct. Ziba Fenton and Esther King.
1812 July 23, Reuben Scott and Mrs. Electa Scott.
" Sept. 17, Sylvester Sears and Persis Hall.
1815 Oct. 5, Allen Bangs and Mrs. Polly Bangs.
1816 June 13, Chester F. Griggs and Lydia King.
" June 20, Ansel Rice and Florilla Smith.
1817 Jan. 30, Israel Crafts and Esther Wells.
" May 29, Hezekiah Warriner Jr. and Hannah Porter.
" July 3, John King and Electa Shattuck.
1818 April 19, Abel Parker and Rhoda Hitchcock.
" Sept. 1, Dennis Bangs and Roana King.
" Oct. 1, Willard Nash and Minerva King.
" Oct. 17, John Hall and Ruth Bangs.
" Dec. 2, Jonas Longley and Almira Crittenden.
1820 Sept. 14, Andrew Ford and Mrs. Olive Baker.
1821 Jan. 31, Chester Hunt and Polly Chamberlin.
" Feb. 28, Jonathan Fuller and Lucinda Leonard.
" Dec. 4, Thaxter Pool and Polly Grout.
1822 March 19, Elisha Atkins and Temperance Claghorn.
" April 21, Benjamin F. Remington and Lydia Rice.
" Sept. 5, Ethan Hitchcock and Mrs. Catharine Lilly.
" Oct. 16, John Joy and Lucy Hitchcock.
1823 May 30, William Bassett and Persis Townsley.
1824 March 3, Ansel Hemenway and Zuba Moody.
" Oct. 7, Ira Holden and Olive Longley.
1825 July 17, Wilder Marsh and Rachel Chamberlin.
" Aug. 26, Lewis Cobb and Elizabeth Holden.
" Nov. 23, Rufus Baker and Rebecca Baker.
1826 Jan. 1, Fitch Wood and Mrs Peggy Hall.
" March 9, Horace White and Harriet Hadlock.
" March 30, Atherton Hunt and Betsey Rogers.

1826 April 9, Alden Sears and Elizabeth Hall.
" April 13, Horace Baker and Mary Ann Curtis.
" May 9, Samuel T. Grout and Laura Joy.
" Oct. 2, Theron Skeels and Samantha King.
" Dec. 21, Simeon Crittenden and Esther Lathrop.
1827 May 17, Phillip Perry and Bathsheba Fuller.
" June 14, Harvey Baker and Ann Eliza Carter.
" Dec. 11, Freeman Atkins and Rebecca Baker.
1828 April 3, Chester Upton and Mermelia Edgarton.
" same, Luther Scott and Rebecca Harmon.
" May 4, Anthony Sears and Lovina Sprague.
1829 Nov. 16, Isaac Atkins and Maria Ford.
1830 May 18, Bardin Damon and Lucy W. Doane.
" Aug. 10, Timothy Baker and Maria Sears.
1831 April 21, Noah Ford and Sophia Ford.
1832 April 4, Ashbel W. Carter and Hannah Joy.
" July 12, Francis Mantor and Mahala Maynard.
" Oct. 25, Levi Harmon and Laura Bartlett.
" " 25, Calvin S. Longley and Eliza Joy.
1833 Simeon Harwood and Sibel Hadlock.
" June, Silas Dodge and Adaline Carrier.
" Aug. 1, Anson Dyer and Mercy Howes.
1834 June 12, Ephriam Baker and Fanny Maria Hawkes.
" Nov. 28, Leonard Marsh and Lois Parker.
1835 Dec. 17, Jonathan Fuller and Mrs. Sophia Hawkes.
" Oct. Levi Holden and Annis Joy.
1836 March 3, Frederick Sears and Rebbecca E. Sears.
" " " Rodolphus Hawkes and Harriet Sears.
" " " Charles Howes and Mary A. Hawkes.
" Oct. 22, Lewis Cobb and Martha Scott.
" Oct. 27, Theophilus Crosby and Abigail C. Thayer.
" " " Horace Thayer and Mary Healy.
1837 June 15, Henry Howes and Lucy Ann Simons.
" July 19, Samuel A. Clark and Clarissa R. Williams.
" Aug. 22, William Hawkes and Tryphosa Lemoin.
1838 Jan. 11, Lewis Bodman and Sylvia H. Longley.
" April 18, Urbane Sears and Mrs. Tryphosa Hawkes.
" Nov. 20, Jeremiah Taylor and Abigail King.
" Dec. 7, Dexter White and Lydia Gurney.
1840 Nov. 26, Amos K. Griggs and Hannah Beals.
" " " Ezra Wood and Martha R. Doane.
1841, Thomas K. Wheeler and Laura Ann Starks.
1842 Sept. 1, Abner Marsh and Loe Rice.
" " " Harvey Danks and Clarissa Rice.

1843 David Thayer and Clarissa Healy.
" Thaddeus Rude and Keziah E. Hall.
" March 29, Erastus Haridon and Sarah C. Rice.
" Oct. Franklin Crittenden and Sarah A. Hitchcock.
" Oct. 16, Nelson Joy and Mahaleth King.
" Dec. 19, William Blood and Eusebia A. Ayres.
1845 May 1, Abner Longley and Abigail King.
1846 March 26, E. Sanderson Carter and Tirzah Stiles.
" May, William R. Thayer and Mary Crowell.
" Nov. 25, Edward S. Coope and Olive B. King.
1847 Nov. 30, Harvey Hadlock and Hannah Hunt.
1848 April 6, Elijah B. Howes and Sarah Jane Simons.
" June 27, Edwin Warriner and Elizabeth V. Crowell.
" Oct. 10, Benjamin Sears and Louisa Atkins.
" Nov. 28, Ira Joy and Hannah Taylor.
" Nov. 30, Feeeman Hamlin and Martha Taylor.
1849 Jan. 23, Wells H. Ayres and Bathsheba Fuller.
1850 Jan. 28, Obed Smith and Mrs. Philena Leonard.
" May 16, Edmund Beals and Eliza Baker.
" July 4, Horace Elmer and Abigail Sears.
1851 July, Nicholas Dubey and Hannah M. Rice.
"   " Sylvester H. Rice and Elizabeth J. Smith.
1853 June 16, Samuel A. Clark and Mrs. Lucy W. Packard.
" Nov. 17, Joshua T. Davis and Harriet S. Harmon.
1854 Jan. 9, Daniel Sears and Susan A. Mansfield.
" Sept. 10, Edwin Scott and Ann Eliza Longley.
" Oct. 3, Albert N. Hubbard and Venila A. Crittenden.
" Nov. 1, Calvin E. Cooley and Olive T. Crittenden.
1855 Feb. 14, Charles H. Rice and Emeline Sears.
" March 18, Dennis W. Baker and Lucretia Vincent.
" May 15, J. Vincent King and Mrs. Ann Elizabeth Church.
" May 23, Lewis Longley and Laura A. Beals.
" Oct. 10, John C. Beals and Lorinda H. Fuller.
" Dec. 24, Franklin H. Beals and Helen C. Deane.
1856 Jan. 10, Apollos H. Gardner and Merila B. Barton.
" July 22, George W. King and Ellen M. Pratt.
" Sept. 16, Asa Holden and Martha E. Hunt.
" Sept. 18, William H. Deming and Mary Ellen Starks.
1857 Feb. 11, Sereno M. Shafner and Luana Brackett.
" April 29, William O. Bassett and Mrs Palixana B. Eldridge.
" June 4, Wilson Gould and Susan Sprague.
1858 May, Willis Vincent and Martha T. Sears.
" July 3, William Sanford Jr. and Margaret Coffin.
" Dec. 2, Levi Holden Jr. and Mrs. Lucy S. Bennett.

1859 June 7, Amos L. Avery and Ellen R. Carter.
" " Thomas W. Mayhew and Sylvia C. Carter.
" Aug. 27, Wm. Onslow Taylor and Hannah M. Crittenden.
" Sept. 8, John H. Bassett and Sylvia H. Longley.
" Sept. 29, Charles B. Mayhew and Mary E. Baker.
1860 May 22, Benjamin Wing and Hannah M. Sears.
" Aug. 22, Spencer N. Tirrell and Eunice Haskins.
" " 29 Welcome E. Whitman and Mrs. Jane Herring.
1861 Jan. 1, Henry A. Howes and Fidelia T. Mantor.
" " 2, Roswell Sears and Mary E. Pierce.
" April 23, Moses M. Mantor and Emily A. Hall.
" May 30, Joseph A. Hitchcock and Emily M. Barnes.
" June 5. Nathaniel Lampson and Carrie E. Longley.
" Sept. 10, B. Parsons Mansfield and Lorinda M. Bartlett.
" Dec. 26, Jesse M. Ward and Ellen J. Harmon.
1862 March 12, Hosea W. Stockwell and Eliza L. Holden.
" Aug. 9, Estes Wilson and Sarah M. Fuller.
" Sept. 4, Henry W. Starks and Emma M. Temple.
1863 Jan. 1, Levi Hawkes and Mrs. Bathsheba Ayres.
" Sept. 29, Mark H. Vincent and Emma A. Brackett.
1864 Aug. 14, Merrick J. Holden and Rebecca C. Mason.
" Nov. 10, A. Dennis Taylor and Fanny L. Starks.
" Dec. 22, Charles L. Anthony and Mary J. Stiles.
1866 June 4, Samuel Williams and Mrs Gratia R. Longley.
" Feb. 21, Henry S. Barton and Bethia H. Sears.
" Nov. 1, Luther Dodge and Ellen J. Hunt.
" Nov. 28, Ambrose K. Sears and Sarah L. Nims.
1867 Jan. 1, Samuel S. Morse and Mary E. Sears.
" May 15, Francis W. Atkins and Lovisa R. Blanchard.
" Nov. 28, Chandler H. Blanchard and Amanda M. Myers.
" Dec. 16, James C. Ritchie and Emma Jane Ayres.
1868 Feb. 29, Aaron G. Ayres and Mrs. Amanda M. Gloyd.
" Sept. 21, Warriner K. Vining and Emily Harwood.
" Dec. 10, Isaac C. Vincent and Delia E. Carter.
" Dec. 28, Lucius Hunt and Sarah E. Holden.
1869 Oct. 28, Lewis E. Harmon and Mrs. Flora G. Crowell.
1870 Feb. 27, Albert E. Marsh and Anna E. Ayres.
" June 22, Charles Crittenden and Julia A. Hall.
1871 April 5, Thomas M. Carter and Flora A. Vincent.
" Sept. 12, Lewis W. Temple and Ella C. Sears.
" Nov. 17, Stillman S. Whitman and Mary E. Brackett.
" " 30, Chester A. Bronson and Flora L. Hunt.
1873 March 3, Lucian A. White and Bessie A. Bennett.
1874 Aug. 23, James H. Eggleston and Sylvia E. Doane.

1874 Aug. 27, Ralph W. Larrabee and Olive E. Hastings.
1875 May 3, William Wallace Cleveland and Julia A. Hawkes.
1878 May 4, Jetson A. Tower and Carrie M. Longley.
" April 9, Walter H. King and Lilly Barge.
" Nov. 28, Herbert L. Crowell and Myrtie Taylor.
" Dec. 28, Wilson Gould and Julia K. Mitchell.
1879 Jan. 1, Dwight A. Hawkes and Ella Mansfield.
" " 15, Theodore Childs and Clara B. Sears.
" March 12, John F. Sprague and Addie M. Roberts.
" Dec. 28, George W. Sears and Jennie H. Houston.
1880 Aug. 25, Dr. Josiah Trow and Mrs. Ellen J. Dodge.
1882 Feb. 1, Wesson E. Mansfield and Mary B. Scott.
" Aug. 19, Lucius Hunt and Hortense A. Mansfield.
" Nov. 18, Clarance A. Hubbard and Addie F. Pierson.
" Dec. 23, Erwin F. Tinney and Flora E. Hewitt.
1883 Jan. 6, Frank E. Mason and Nellie U. White.
" March 4, Charles H. Maynard and G. Etta Fuller.
" Dec. 25, Adna C. Bissell and Florence B. Scott.
1885 Melvin H. White and Sarah Ida Stiles.
" Wm. H. Hawkes and Mrs. Martha J. Stiles.
1886 May 6, Newell Dyer and Lila R. Thayer.
" July 6, Erastus Graves and Maria H. Underwood.
" Sept. 25, Dallas Staples and Clara B. Thompson.
Nov. 13, Frederick N. Haskins and Elizabeth B. Horton.
" Dec. 30, S. Jerome Cornwell and Florence E. Taylor.
1887 Jan. 29, Charles W. Hawkes and Carrie B. Holden.
" Feb. 1, Clarence Gould and Etta Jenks.

DEATHS.

The town records contain very meagre and incomplete records of deaths for many of the first years of the town's history, being occasionally one inserted among the record of births. The following is mainly from the diary of Mrs. Jerusha King, and is also imperfect, as in some cases the Christian name is lacking. But as the best record attainable for at least a part of the time it covers, we accept it. The figures following the name in some instances, is the age.

1827.

Jan. 14, Capt. Luther Rice's child, same day, Russell Hunt's child, Feb. 18, Elisha Clark's child, March 26, old Mr. Hunt, April 15, William Patch's child, May 11, Horace White's child, July 23, Elijah Marsh's child, July 29, Miss Baker, Oct., Andrew Ford's two children, Nov. 7, Mrs. Bangs.

1828.

Jan. 1, William Ward's child, March 12, William Putney's child, Mar. 16, Esq. Zenas Bangs, April 2, Asa Thayer, May 1, Mr. Sprague's child, July 10, Mr. Holden's child, July 15, John Damon's child, Aug. 18, Amasa Howard's child, Aug. 19, Chester Smith's child, Aug. 20, Amasa Howard's child, Aug. 27, Ezra Brackett's child, Aug. 28, Ziba Pool's child, Sept. 8, Milton Goodspeed's child, Sept. 9, Mrs. Moses Chamberlin, same day, Mrs. Ziba Pool, Sept. 10, Mr. Howes, Sept. 27, Simeon Crittenden's child, Sept. 29, Mrs. Roland Sears, Sept. 30, Mr. Roland Sears, Nov. 12, Mrs. Lascombe, Dec. 5, Phebe Baker. No. deaths, 21.

1829.

Jan. 3, Andrew Pool, Jan. 27, Theophilus Crosby's child, Feb. 1, Mr. Ward,s child, Feb. 10, Clarissa Chamberlin, 22, April 11, Jesse Hall, May 30, Mrs. Solomon Graves, June 5, Samuel Dickinson's child, July 3, Mr. Wing's child, Aug. 27, Mrs. Pratt, Sept. 11, Mrs. Vining, Oct. 18, old Mrs. Hitchcock, Oct. 27, Edmund Longley, 3d, Nov. 13, old Mrs Pierce, Dec. 18, Edwin Lathrop. No. of deaths, 14.

1830.

Jan. 9, Mrs. Baker, and Mr. Look, April——,Moses Manter, and Almira Dodge, May 1, Alvin Sears' child, - — Dea. Hammond, July 12, Mrs. Robinson, Aug. 21, Shubael Fuller's child, Aug. 25. Edward Crowell's child, Aug. 26, Elijah Marsh, Sept. 26, widow Elias Rice, Sept. 28, Moses Chamberlin, Dec. 15, Chester Hunt's child, Dec. 15, and 21, two children of Quartus Taylor. No. of deaths, 15.

1831.

Jan. 9, Mr. Haskin's two children, Jan. 11, Sally Smith, Jan. 13, Reuben Scott's child, Jan. 17, Julia Bartlett, Jan. 18, Warren Robinson's child, Jan. 30, Abigail Bartlett, Feb. 4, Quartus Taylor's child, same day, Ezekiel Edgarton's child, Feb. 8, Mr. Davis' child, Feb. 9, Jonathan Damon's child, same day, Chester Smith, Feb. 20, Mr. Lascombe, March 5, Mrs. Rice, March 13, Erastus Hitchcock, May 11. Fitch Wood's child, May 28, Deacon Newton, July 19, William Sanford, Aug. 2, Mrs. Mantor, Sept. 15, Mr. Hulbert's child, Sept. 20, Silas Lilley, Oct. 21, Mr. Putney's child, Nov. 25, Mrs. Sophia Ford, Dec. 22, Mr. Crowell, Dec. 23, Harriet Healy, 18. No. of deaths, 25.

1832.

Feb. 7, Samuel Nims, Feb. 18, Mrs. Baker, Feb. 22, Mrs. Longley, March 3, Mrs. Smith, March 14, Mrs. Hall, March 19, Mr. Densmore's child, March 23, E. Crowell's child, April 1, Elisha Robinson's child, April 2, Mr. Curtis' child, May——, Mr. Harmon's child, May 10, widow Thayer, June 10, Dea. Hall, June 11, Luther Longley, June 15, Mr. Carter, July——, Mr. Pierce's child, Sept. 20, Jonas King, Oct. 19, Edmund Hawks, Dec. 14, Edward Porter's child. No. of deaths. 19.

1833.

Jan. 19, old Mr. Sears, Feb.— Alvin Sears Jr.'s child, April—, widow Lilly, Mrs. Sprague, and Amanda Howard, July—, Catharine Lilly, Sept. 17, Mrs. Jonathan Fuller, Oct.—, old Mrs. Field, Oct. 31, Mrs. Howard, Nov. 1, Eliza Ann Fuller, and Mary Ann Leonard, Nov. 2, Burdin Damon's child, Nov. 11, John Hadlock Jr., Nov. 22, Mrs. Milton Leonard, Dec. 1', Mrs. Jonathan Fuller Jr. No. of deaths, 15, five of which were in the house of Jonathan Fuller.

1834.

Feb —, Mr. Atkins' child, and Mr. Wing's child, Feb. 23, Mrs. Loveland, March 13, Joel Bartlett, April 27, Elijah Marsh Jr., Apr. 29, Sarah, adopted daughter of John King, 10, May 2, Mr. Mansfield's child, May 20, old Mrs. Longley, Sept. 8, John Braymon's child, Oct. 7, Mrs. Mansfield, Oct.——, Harvey Baker's child, Nov. 1, Amanda Smith, Nov. 8, Dea. Spafford, Nov. 12, and 14, two children of Mr. Barckett, Dec.——, Salome Goodspeed. No. of deaths, 17.

1835.

Jan. 20, Cushing Shaw's child, Feb.—Mr. Wing's child, Mr. Carter's child, Sears, Mr. Howard, March 1, Mr. Wing, March 7, Mr. Hill, Mar. 29, Mr. Vining, April 19, Chester Griggs' child, May 9, Mr. Pierce's child, June 6, Rev. Jonathan Grout, 73, June 23, Mrs. Smith, July 19, Rebecca Smith, July 25, Mr. Brackett, Aug. 9, Joel Vincent, Oct. 10, Joseph Howes Jr., Nov. 21, Freeman Atkins' child, Dec. 10, Mr. Holden's child, Dec.——, Mrs. Edgarton, Dec. 29, Mrs. Doane. Deaths, 20.

1836.

March 6, Cornelia Curtis, 18, April 3, old Mr. Baker, April 4, Mr. Damon, May 12, Achsah Hall, July 8, Joseph Longley Sen., Aug. 19, — Mantor, Dec. 22, — Holden's child. No. of deaths, 7.

1837.

Feb. 21, old Mrs. Tobey, March 18, Taylor Grout's child, March 19, Millo Carter's wife, May 21, Dea. Lathrop, June 12, Martha Marsh, 22, July 10, Marila Beals, 4, Aug. 4, Sylvia King, 16, Aug. 15, Elijah Longley's child, Sept. 10, — Barnard. Sept. 28, Abraham Parker, Oct. Lydia Lilley, Oct. 8, E. Hawkes, Oct. 26, William Hawkes, Oct. 27, Washburne Hall, Oct. 31, Theodore Marsh, 22, Oct. — William Cudworth's child. Nov. 30, Elisha Hunt, Dec. 5, Ezekiel Edgarton, Dec. 15, Phebe Newton. No. of deaths, 19.

1838.

Feb. 27, Noah Baker, May 28, Mr. Doane, Aug. 8, old Mrs. Cooley, Sept. 12, C. Crosby's two children, Oct. 23, Mrs. Lysander Pelton, Oct. ——, widow E. Marsh, Dec. 23, Esther Grout. No. of deaths, 8.

1839.

Jan. 12, widow Thayer, Jan. 27, Emory Rice, Feb. 15, Mrs. Andrew Wood, Feb. 19, Polly Hall, Mrs. Jonas King, 59, Feb. 28, Mr. Ives, Mar. 2, Mr. Warriner, March 13, Lydia Hall, March 12, Mr. Porter's child, March 22, Edmund Hawkes' son, March 30, Mrs. Alden Sears, April 1, Calvin Longley's child, May 25, widow Rice's daughter, July 3, Mrs. Stephen Damon, July 13, Amos King, 81, Sept. 18, Mr. Burton, Oct. 8, Abigail Rood, 18, Oct. 10, another child of Rufus Rood, Oct. 16, Lois Joy, Oct. 28, Luther Scott's child, Nov. 13, Andrew Wood, Dec. 16, Jonas Holden. No. of deaths, 22.

1840.

March 29, Rev. Tyler Thatcher's wife, April 25, John Taylor, June 13, old Mrs. Sears, July 23, Calvin Longley's child, Aug. 14, Allen Bassett's child. No. of deaths, 5.

1841.

Jan. 24, Russell Hunt's child, April 17, Dea. Hammond, June 12, Ezra Wood, July 5, Lucretia Parker, July 15, Mr Olds' child, Sept. 23, widow Lathrop, Oct. 17, Rebecca Sears, Oct. 28, Rhoda Harmon, 22, Alanson Hitchcock, Nov. 2, Fanny Curtis, Nov. 18, Mr. Olds, Nov. 27, Mrs. Joel Baker, Dec. 6, Ezra King, 57. No. of deaths, 13.

1842.

Jan. 9, Charlotte Crosby, 20, Jan. 21, old Mrs. Harmon, Jan. 27, Edwin Streeter's child, and old Mrs. Dodge, May 3, Mrs. Jonas Holden, May 7, Jackson Cook's child, June 4, Levi Harmon's child, Aug. 18, Joshua Vincent, Nov. 18, Stephen Damon, Dec. 12, Edmund Longley Esq., Dec. 19, Mrs. Ethan Hitchcock. No. of deaths, 11.

1843.

Jan. 5, Mr. Mc Coy, Jan. 13, Hezekiah Warriner, Jan. 31, Otis Longley's child, Feb. 16, old Mrs. Ford, May 11, Millo Carter's child, May 23, Col. Noah Joy, Aug. ——, Mrs. Ebenezer Crosby, Sept. 13, Mrs. Ebenezer Crowell, July 5, Jonas Longley, Sept. 26, Chillingsworth Crosby's child, Oct. 2, old Mrs. Brackett, Oct. 3, Elizabeth Crosby, 23, Nov. 4, old Mrs. Hitchcock. No. of deaths, 13.

1844.

Jan. 9, Mrs Oliver Patch, Feb. —— Olive Hawkes, March 5, Elisha Cobb's child, same day Harvey Baker's child, March 30. Rev. Anson Dyer's child, same day, —— Barrus' child, April 2, old Mr. Scott, Apr. 18, David Carrier's child, May 28, Lois Hitchcock, July 30, Dudley Hitchcock, Oct. 2, James Mantor's child, Oct. 25, Mrs. Ephraim Marsh, Oct. ——, Roland Sears' child, Nov. 27, Almira Elmer, Dec. 23, Mr. Burt's child. No. of deaths, 15.

1845.

Jan. 1, Roswell Baker's child, May——, old Mrs. Howard, and Esther Maynard, June 17, Dea. Tobey, July 17, Chester Hunt, Oct.——, Lydia Sears, Dec. 27, Jonas Rice, 90. No. of deaths, 7.

1846.

Jan. 1, Harvey Baker's son, March——, Atherton Hunt's child, April 1, widow Taylor, and widow Scott, April 23, Franklin Crittenden, May 7, Sylvanus Rice's wife and child, May 21, J. W. King's child, Nov.—— Mrs. Loomis, Calley Holden, Nov. 24, Elijah Longley's child. 11 in No.

1855.

Jan. 5. Mrs. Wood, Jan. 10, old Mrs. Campbell, 95, March 24, Margaret Hawkes, April 20, Benjamin Sears, May 4 Moses Blood, May 20, Mrs. Jonathan Damon, do. Ann Cornelia Wood, 11. June——, Chester Smith, 85, July 30, Stillman Sears, 23, Aug. 3, Thomas K. Wheeler's child, Aug. 5, Mrs. Williams, Aug. 11, Ebenezer Sears' child, Nov. 27, Jane M. Ford, Dec. 11, Louisa Doane. No. of deaths, 14.

1856.

Feb. 14, Dennis Baker's child, March 5, Mrs. David Thayer, Mar. 6, Lemuel Eldridge, April 26. Ruth Scott, July——, Leman Vining's child, July 13, Ethan Hitchcock's son, Aug. 24, Vienna Sears, Sept. 15, Betsey Sanford, Nov. 6, Dea. Rufus Sears, Nov. 23, Mrs. Fitch Wood, Dec. 25, old Mr. Dodge, Apr. 30, Olive Scott. No. of deaths, 12.

1857.

Jan. 11, Mrs. Daniel Hall, Jan. 17, Mrs. Levi Holden, Jan. 30, Joseph Howes, March 15, Oliver Shattuck, April ——, Mrs. Thomas Longley, June 15, Uzziel Simons, Sept. 10, Mrs. Philena Turner, Oct. 22, Mrs. Martha Taylor, Dec. ——, Mrs. Elisha Clark. No. of deaths, 9.

1858.

Jan. 3, Preserved Larrabee's child, Feb. 26, Matilda Damon, Mar. 6, Mrs. Ichabod Hawkes, April 12, Calvin S. Longley, April 16, Perlina Harmon, May 1, David Vining, June 1, David Vining's daughter, Aug. 18, Harlan H. Rice, 16, drowned, Aug——, Joseph Tobey, Sept. 18, Silas King, Nov. 27, Mrs. John C. Beals, 21, Dec. 21, Mrs. Amos King, 92, April 5, Mr. Morton's child, Dec. 27, widow Crosby.   14 deaths.

1859.

March 18, Mrs. Alpheus Hawkes, March 30, Hepsey Hall, April ——, Leonard Marsh's child, June 9, wife of Dea. Smith, Sept. 5, Caroline Holden, same day, Jonathan Damon's son. No. of deaths, 6.

1860.

Jan. 14, Mrs. Tyler Curtis, Jan. 15, J. M. Parker's child, Jan. 24, Mr. Gould's child, May 15, Mrs. Hollister Baker, June 9, Sylvanus Rice, June 13, Phebe Damon, Aug. 28, Edwin Scott's child, same day, Roswell Baker's child, Sept. 27, William Bassett, Oct. 6, Ebenezer Wood, Nov. 16, widow Batchelder. No. of deaths, 11.

1861.

Jan. 17, Ephraim Marsh, Feb. 6, Thomas Eldridge's child, April 16, Mrs. Mitchell, April 18, Mrs. Mantor, June 23, Ruth Atkins, 92, June 25, Wells Ayres, Aug. 6, —— Curtis, Aug. 29, Mrs. Taylor Grout, Nov. 11, Almon Atkins, 25, Dec. 20, Charles Mayhew, Dec. 26, Nathaniel Hall, Dec. 27, widow of Rev. Jonathan Grout. No. of deaths, 12.

1862.

Jan. 19, Lewis Sears' child, Feb. 16, Rhoda Scott, May —, Mrs. Porter Hawkes, May 16, Ellen, wife of Wm. H. Deming, 22, June 1, Mrs. Levi Hawkes, July 6, Melissa Eldridge, July 11, Mr. Mitchell's daughter, July 16, Elisha Clark, Aug. 21, Peter L. Baker's child, Aug. 23, Emma Wheeler, Sept. 1, Mrs. Eddy, Sept. 8, George Lathrop, Sept. 13, widow Cooley, Sept. 28, Polly Rood, Oct. 3, Elijah B. Howes' child, Nov. ——, Urbane Sears 2d. No. of deaths, 16.

1863.

Jan. 8, Thomas Hall, a soldier, Feb. 20, widow Silas King, March —, Warham Stiles, March 25, Clark Sprague, June 12, widow John King, June 13, Mrs. John Taylor, July 6, Aaron Ayres' child, July 26, Mrs. Aaron Ayres, July 29, Mrs. Reuben Scott, Geo. C. Brayman, Noah Baker, Henry Mason, and George Clark died in the army, Sept. 13, Mrs. Garner Stiles, Sept. 5. Edmund Longley, Sept. 20, William Sanford's child, Oct. 11, old Mrs. Stiles, Oct. 13, Hollister Baker, Oct. 29, widow Alvin Sears, Nov. —, Mr. Rogers, a soldier, Dec. 4, Henry Hunt a soldier, Dec. 15, Chapman Parker, Dec. 20, Levi Hawkes' child. 23 deaths.

1864.

Jan. 2, Milison Turner, Jan. 9, John Brown's child, Feb. 9, Elijah B. Howes' child, March 1, Nathan Vincent, April 29, Thankful Damon, May 25, old Mrs. Sears, June 23, Mrs. Lyman Rice, Aug. 31, Joseph Hitchcock's child, Sept. 30, old Mrs. Thorp, Nov—, Mrs. Hayden. 10.

1865.

Jan. 27, Mr Patch, Feb. 15, Hannah Crosby, April 16, Theodore Field June 29, Mrs. J. Monroe Parker, Aug. 25, Mrs. Williams, Aug. 26, old Mrs. Hunt, Sept. 12, Horace White, Sept. 24, Sally Snow, Oct. 2, Mrs. Hale, Oct. 22, Willis Vincent's child, Oct. 28, Mrs. Moses Rice. 11.

1866.
March 25, old Mrs. Fales, April 7, Mrs. Anthony Sears, May 19, John Taylor, May 20, Ethan Hitchcock, June 4, Mrs. Consider Smith, Aug. 28, Mary Holden, Sept. 18, Esther Hall, Dec. 5, Levi Holden Sr. 99, Dec. 7, Mrs. Esther Longley, 90. No. of deaths, 9.

1867.
Jan. 1, Dea. Simeon Crittenden, Jan. 5, Mrs. Luther Scott, March 6, Mrs. Freeman Atkins, 62, March 19, Edward Lewis Crowell, 37, May 2, Mrs. John Starks, 84, May 15, Mrs. Erastus Kinney, May 16, Mrs. Nathan Clark, and Willard Carpenter's child, July 19, Thos. Eldridge s child, July 22, Jonathan Brackett, Aug. 7, widow of Sylvanus Rice, Aug. 10, old Mrs. Hitchcock, Sept. 10. Daniel Rice, about 90, Sept. 20, Erastus Kinney' child, Oct. 8, Mrs. Proctor Marsh, Oct. 18, Charles Baker, Nov. 16, Lewis Cobb, Dec. 24, widow Daniel Rice.   Deaths, 18.

1868.
Jan. 16, widow Temperance Harmon, Feb. 3, Mrs. John Starks, 83, Feb. 4, Calvin Scott, Feb. 14, Mrs. Benjamin Sears, 40, April 12, Mr. Gilbert, April 18, Mrs Jonathan Fuller, May 26, Simeon Hitchcock, July 5, Onslow Taylor's child, Aug. 1, Mrs. Gillett's child, Oct. 25, Zebedee Wood, Oct. 26, Sylvester Rice's child, Dec. 24, widow Joseph Howes. No. of deaths, 12.

1869.
Feb. 25, Edward Warriner, 20, March 25, Nettie Hall, 13, April 22, Alonzo Turner's child, July 27, Mrs. Eri Hitchcock, Aug. 4, William Sanford, Oct——, a French child. No. of deaths, 6.

1870.
Jan. 25, Mr. Stone's child, Feb. 11, Benjamin Sears, 48, same day Mrs. Bushnell, 73, Feb. 22, E. P. Hunt's child, March 13, Willard Carpenter's child, May 21, Reuben Scott Jr., 47, June 25, John V. King, 47, Aug. 16, Daniel Crosby, 58, Aug. 21, Justin Wood's child, Aug.— Gilbert Gould's child, Oct. 20, widow Polly Hunt, 75, Dec. 23, Polly Baker, 86.   No. of deaths, 12.

1871.
Jan. 23, Mrs. Joshua Williams, 48, Jan. 28, Abner Gurney's child, March 27, George Doane, 33, March 28, Garner Stiles, 66, May 16, Gilbert Gould's child, Nov. 20, Edward Crowell, 77.   No. of deaths, 6.

1872.
Jan. 20, James Doane. 65, March 11, Ira Turner, 9, Mar. 16, William Thayer's child, April 8, John H. Wood, 79, April 9, Warriner Vining's child, June 3, Mrs. Elias Rice 87, Sept. 21, Mrs. Abraham Parker, 88, Oct. 21, Mrs. Nathan Tyler, 40, Nov. 17, Mrs. Reuben Crittenden, 65, Nov. 24, George Goddard's child, Dec. 12, Nathen Clark's child, Dec. 13, Alvin Kinney, 79,   No. of deaths, 12.

1873.
Jan. 27, Eliza Guilford, 22, March 4, John Vincent, 70, April 12, Rowland Stiles' child, April 15, Dennis Taylor's child, July 7. Seth Hayden, 83, July 16, Anthony Sears, 68, Dec. 4, Mrs. Dea. Eldridge 82, Dec. 7, Sally Wood, 75. No. of deaths, 8.

1874.
Jan. 29, Elijah Shaw's child, Feb. 14, Harvey Baker, 70, Feb. 27, Ichabod Hawkes, 84, May 28, Martha D. Wood, 80, same day, Mrs. Mary Blodgett, 25, June 8, Charles Baker, 58, Sept. 10, widow Vincent King, 50. No. of deaths, 7.

1875.
March 4, Mrs. Chapin, 88, March 23, W. Simons, 84, April 6, Urbane Sears, 61, April — Lucius Hunt's child, May 5, Dea. Eldridge, 91. 5

1876.
March 26, Mrs. Horton, April 20, Mrs. John Vincent, 74, April 27, Alvah Stiles, Aug. 1, Mrs. Rufus Sprague, 70, Aug. 15, Porter Hawkes' son, suicided, Dec ——, Porter Hawkes, Reuben Scott, 86. 7

1877.
Jan. 4. Samuel Thayer, 89, Jan. 22, Mrs. Sarah Brackett, 80, Jan. 25, Dea. Samuel Hall, 76, Feb. 27, Warriner King, 90, July 17, Mrs. Lucy M. Gillett, 74, July 18, Mrs. Susan S. Gould, 40, July 28, Bertha A. Simpson, Aug. 18, Mrs. Jane Maynard, 41, Sept. 20, Mrs. Betsey Kinney, 83, Oct. 4, Frederick Hubbard. No. of deaths, 10.

1878.
March 12, Lucretia Bassett, March 21, Mrs. Sarah Hunt, April 13, Luther Dodge, Aug. 4, Lottie J. Andrews, Sept. 15, Harvey Stiles, 42, Nov. 2, Zachary Hall, 87, Dec. 22, Ruth M. Rice. No. of deaths, 7.

1879.
March 9, Mrs. Polly Crittenden, Aug. 21, Daniel Hall, Oct. 17, Mrs. Apphia Crowell, Nov. 29, Clark Sears, Nov. 30, Freeman Atkins, 73, Dec. 19, Mrs. Lucinda Gould, 73. No. of deaths, 6.

1880.
Jan. 24, Clinton H. Hadlock, April 14, Harriet M. Sears, April 19, Martin Vining, May 7, Hattie L. Luce, Jan. 6, Mrs. Permelia S. Meacham, Aug. 28, Bela Mitchell, Sept. 10, Sarah Clark Mason, July 28, Reuben Crittenden, Nov. 3, Waldo K. Baker, Dec. 1, Mrs. Cordelia B. Doane. No. of deaths, 10.

1881.

Feb. 4, Kate A. Eldridge, March 8, Jane R. Mansfield, March 15, Emeline T. Dodge, April 1, Erastus Mansfield, April 29, Augusta E. Maynard, May 21, Edward M. Field, June 5, Clara Belle Sears, June 20, Abraham Parker, Oct. 9, Rufus C. Sprague, Nov. 3, Bartholomew Scanlan, Sept. 18, Susanna Mansfield.   No of deaths, 12.

1882.

March 15, Mrs. Betsey R. Hunt, 83, May 22, Mrs. Julia A. Crittenden, 34, May 25, Francis H. King, Dec. 5, Mrs. Gracia R. Williams, Dec. 16, Jonathan Fuller, 90, Dec. 17, Nelson Brackett. No. of deaths 7.

1883.

Jan. 1, Joanna H. Clark, Jan. 21, Arthur A. Turner, Feb. 2, Thaddeus Wood, April 8, Mrs. Abigail Fuller, June 2, Mehitable Stafford, July 28, Emeline Stetson, Aug. 6, Anna Vincent, Aug. 13, Mrs. Harriet White, 84, Sept. 26, Flora A. Gould, 19.   No. of deaths, 9.

1884.

Jan. 7, Heman Hitchcock, 84, March 5, Sarah Brayman, Aug. 4, Jessie Staples, June 19, Olive Holden, Oct. 17, Erastus W. Brayman, Josiah Archie Barber.   No. of deaths, 6.

1885.

Aug. 18, Carrie E. King. Sept. 11, Henry A. Hillman, Sept. 17, Luther Scott, Sept. 22, Ellen Graves, Nov. 10, Lucy Scott, Nov. 21, Lucius Scott. Nov. —, Cora M. Turner, Dec. 12, Henry W. King.   8.

1886.

March 19, Horace Dwight Seymour, 24, April 19, Bertie E. Galbraith, 6, May 21, Carrie L. Scott, 16, Aug. 20, Leroy G. Carrier, 4 mos. Aug. 23, Levi Holden, 79, Oct. 9. Silas Dodge, 81, Nov. 6, Sanderson E. Carter, 69, Nov. 21, Ira Holden, 88, Dec. 14, Ira Joy, 87, Dec. 17, Arron Gould, 80, Dec. 27, Norman Phillip Kenney, 6 mos., April 15, Wealthy B. Howes, 18.   No. of deaths, 12.

A record has been furnished, showing that the cemetery in the old sixth district was opened in 1827, and that Capt. Luther Rice's child was the first buried there. The record gives the names of 57 buried there, and having been abandoned several years ago, it is evident that nearly a hundred have been buried there.

MISCELLANIES.

The following record of a meeting of the inhabitants of No. 7, bearing date Feb. 24, 1778, is furnished by Geo. D. Crittenden, having been left in an account book kept by Zebedee Wood, before and after his coming to Hawley. It will be noticed that the date is fourteen years before the incorporation of the town, and it appears that Mr. Wood was clerk of the meeting. The record is given to show the customs adopted by the pioneer settlers, and the disadvantages under which they lived.

Feb. 24, 1778; At a town meeting held at the house of Samuel Hitchcock, Thomas King, Moderator: Voted Nathaniel Rudd, Samuel Hitchcock and Thomas King a committee to get the town salt and distribute the same.

Voted, they will do nothing about getting a town stock of powder and lead.

Voted, Thomas King to go and talk with the proprietors and see what they will do about building mills and getting on the rest of the settlers.

Voted Thomas King, Daniel Burt and Nathaniel Rudd committee men to go and see after a council.

Voted to hire preaching this year, and to raise money by subscription to pay the same.

Voted Nathaniel Rudd to draw up a paper and get signers.

Voted to hire Mr. Sherwin to preach.

Voted David Parker to agree with him.

Voted Samuel Hitchcock, Silas Hitchcock and Nathaniel Parker committee men to lay out a highway from Mr. Curtis' to the grant.

Copy of a subscription paper for the support of a school:—

We, whose names are hereunder signed, being disposed to have a school amongst us the ensuing winter, hereby bind ourselves to pay the following sums affixed to our names, provided we can pay the same in the products of the earth. Furthermore, agreed to have Mr. Nash keep an exact account of every day each scholar comes, and if any subscriber in the district does not subscribe his proportion according to what he sends, hereby obligate ourselves to make it up according to what we do send.

Zebedee Wood,	13 shillings,
Nathan West,	8 "
Jacob Hunt,	10 "
Zebulon Benton,	7 "
Zephaniah Lathrop,	7 "
Ichabod Hawkes,	8 "

In 1865, there were living in the old seventh district, which then numbered a population of about 70, thirteen persons who were over 70, eleven being over 75, seven over 80, and one over 90. An issue of the Greenfield Gazette in December of that year gave their names and ages, and we reproduce it, with the addition of the date of death and age.

Ethan Hitchcock,	92	died	May 30, 1866,	aged	93
Mrs. Esther Longley,	89	"	Dec. 7, 1886,	"	90
Daniel Rice,	88	"	Sept. 10, 1867,	"	90
Mrs. Sarah Rice,	87	"	Dec. 24, 1867,	"	89
John Taylor,	84	"	May 13, 1866,	"	85
John Starks,	82	"	May 2, 1867,	"	84
Mrs. Anne Starks,	80	"	Feb. 3, 1868,	"	83
Mrs. Polly Crittenden,	79	"	March 19, 1879,	"	92
Warriner King,	78	"	Feb. 27, 1877,	"	90
Mrs. Jerusha King,	77	"	May 30, 1882	"	93
Zachary Hall,	75	"	Nov. 2, 1878,	"	87
Jonathan Fuller,	73	"	Dec. 16, 1882,	"	90
Mrs. Pamelia Fuller,	73	"	April 18, 1868,	"	76

Copy of a record from an account book kept by Warriner King.

Hawley, Nov. ye 6, 1811.

Then reckoned and settled all accounts with John Starks from the beginning of the world to this date.

Warriner King.
John Starks.

On the occasion of the marriage of Rev. Jonathan Grout, Oct. 23, 1795 he made a large register or certificate, neatly and elaborately done in pen printing, at the bottom of which is the following, written as an acrostic:—

Man placed in paradise to live,
And formed and aimed for social bliss,
Rejoiced when God a helpmeet gave,
Received and owned her, bone of his.
In this connection, would men gain
All joy which thence might sweetly flow,
Good acts reciprocal must prove,
Each in their turn should kindness show.

This sheet is in the possession of Mr. Grout's granddaughter, Mrs. C. A. Stebbins, of Deerfield, also two sermons delivered by Mr. Grout, printed in pamphlet form, one on the occasion of a Fourth of July celebration in Heath, in 1803, the other at the close of a singing school in Cummington in March, 1811. She has other relics from the ancestral homestead, also some articles from the Grout family are placed in Memorial Hall.

An Illinois paper of Jan. 14, 1887, reproduces a copy of a poem written as a letter by Jedediah Lathrop to his brother Thomas. It was originally written April 27, 1829, when he was a clerk in a store, and he dwells at length upon the anticipation of the opening of spring.

The life and character of Zachary Hall demands a space in this work. He originated from Ashfield, and in childhood was said to possess an average amount of intellect, but sometime in early life he became demented to a certain extent, and in consequence, became an object of charity, and came upon the town of Hawley. One account says that the cause of his downfall was a religious excitement under which he labored at one time in his youth. For many years he lived with Otis Longley, but upon the purchase of the Town farm in 1851, he was removed there and passed the rest of his life there. He had many halluciuations, some people believing his abilities were better than he assumed, and that his peculiarities were put on for effect. He once had a sound tooth extracted, saying that it once bit his mother, and cut off one of his fingers because it pinched her. Sometimes he would decorate himself in every conceivable style and color of patches on his clothing, sometimes sewing on birch bark. He usually wore a handkerchief tied over his head, as he said, to keep the flies out of his ears. He often spent hours at a time killing flies, by striking them with a little paddle or narrow shingle, and was a pretty good shot. Occasionally some particular shrub or weed would be the object of his contempt, and he would spend days in destroying all he could find of that particular species.

One Fourth of July he heated water and put on the Canada thistles which grew in the chip yard near the house. It had the effect of wilting the noxious thistles at the time, but whether the treatment effected a permanent eradication, we are not informed. He was usually harmless, but at times his vagaries assumed a mischievous character, for instance, he once made a yard in an isolated part of the pasture and shut the cows in it, so they were not readily found. A large number of mud of swallows annually built nests and reared their young under the eaves of the barn and a long shed. One Sunday when the family had gone to church, he knocked down the nests and destroyed the eggs and young birds. Sometimes he was coaxed, and sometimes threatened into submission. At one time he had a severe attack of jaundice, and on asking the proprietor what made his skin so yellow, he was gravely informed that it was caused by his smoking, whereupon he laid by his pipe and never used it again. Meetings were frequently held in the school house in that neighborhood, and one Sunday morning, the minister being late, he took his seat in the desk and quietly remained until the minister arrived, when he as quietly vacated it.

Sometimes he would run away from home, and on one of these occasions, one of the town fathers told him the town bought the farm for his special use, and he must stay and take care of it, which had the desired effect. A long chapter might be written on his eccentricities, but enough has been said to give a good description. Suffice it to say that he lived much beyond the allotted age of man, and it is believed that he enjoyed life, in his way, to an average degree. It is said in his last sickness he realized his condition, and was much more composed at the approach of death than many another He died Nov. 2, 1878, aged 87.

In the early years of the town's history, old Mr. Hale lived a little north of the South Hawley post office. He lived a kind of hermit life by himself, and had some peculiar fancies, among which was the supposition that he was tormented by evil spirits, and would show fight with his supposed enemies, armed with a pitchfork.

Joseph P. Manning, an eccentric man, lived in Ashfield, and owned thirty acres of land now on the farm of Joseph Hitchcock in Hawley, on which was a small house where he often stayed for a month at a time, sometimes keeping his cow there. Most people in Hawley who were living thirty years ago will remember him as a kind of local celebrity. He spent much of his time travelling about, carrying a bag of lime and a whitewash brush, occasionally getting a job of whitewashing, having favorite places where he would call for a "dish of tea." He was very erratic in his religious convictions, and sometimes his voice could be heard a mile when he was at his devotions.

The year 1816 was remarkable for its cold summer. It is said that spots could be seen on the sun. Severe frosts occurred every month; June 7th and 8th snow fell, and it was so cold that crops were cut down, even freezing the roots, but they were replanted. In the early Autumn when corn was in the milk it was so thoroughly frozen that it never ripened and was scarcely worth harvesting. Breadstuffs were scarce and prices high and the poorer class of people were often in straits for want of food. It must be remembered that the granaries of the great west had not then been opened to us by railroad communication, and people were obliged to rely upon their own resources or upon others in their immediate locality.

The winter and spring of 1857 presented some peculiar freaks. In February, a succession of thaws, resembling April weather, carried off nearly all the snow, and considerable maple sugar was made.

March did not betray its trust, furnishing the usual complement of cold, snow and wind. April 20 and 21, the ground having been previously bare, a snow storm raged for about thirty-six hours, leaving fully three feet of solid snow on the ground. Travelling was impossible for several days, and it was believed that had the weather been cold and the snow dry, it would have been six feet deep.

Two notable thunder showers passed over the town within a year of each other. Aug. 18, 1858, near the close of an intensely hot day, a shower passed from southwest to northeast, accompanied with a wind which assumed the proportions of a tornado, and forests, orchards and buildings were demolished through a narrow strip where the wind was most violent. On the evening of July 2, 1859, a terrific thunderstorm of considerable duration occurred. The damage in this case was caused by water, many of the highways being literally torn in pieces.

The town received its full complement of damage and subsequent expenses by the memorable flood which swept like a tidal wave over New England, Oct. 4, 1869.

The early inhabitants were sometimes in terror in consequence of the prevalence of beasts of prey. It is related of the wife of Timothy Baker that at times when her husband was absent from home, it was her custom to shut her children in the house when going after the cow, to prevent their straying from the house and being devoured by wild beasts.

Warriner King when a small boy, went to his grandfather's house, about two miles from home, and not returning as soon as expected, his father went after him; meeting him on the way, and not wishing to reveal the object of his mission or the fears he entertained for his little son's safety, he coolly asked him if he had seen anything of their sheep.

In the spring of 1834, the following families removed from Hawley, the most of them going to Ohio:— Solomon Graves, John Hadlock, Rev. John Breed and Elder Wagner. At that time the "Western Reserve," or "New Connecticut," in Ohio, was just opened and was an objective point to many emigrating west.

April 20, 1856, the families of Luther Rice, Calvin Rice and Nicholas Dubey removed west, several members of the family having preceded them. Sept. 5, 1857, their parents, Capt. Luther Rice and wife went to join them.

A few years after the marriage of Ansel Rice, he moved with his family to Ohio, going the entire distance with an ox team, with which he carried his family and some furniture. A cow was tied to the wagon, which furnished milk during the journey. The family usually slept in the wagon, occasionally putting up at a private house. On the morning of their departure, their neighbors for quite a distance assembled to leave parting congratulations, making as much capital of the event as a presidential party would at the present day.

At the organization of the first Sunday school in June, 1820, Thomas Longley was superintendent, and among the teachers were Dea. Lathrop, Levi Eldridge, Ezra King, Theophilus Crosby, Judah Crosby, Fitch Wood, Joshua Longley. Noah Joy was clerk; his duties being to keep a record of the scripture verses committed and recited by each scholar. The reward was a four page tract for each forty verses repeated. A few years later, question books were introduced, and a library added.

John Hadlock was a carpenter, and for a large part of the time was away from home in the pursuit of that vocation. On a frosty evening in the fall of the year, when on his way home, in passing over a lonely portion of the way, he saw what he imagined to be a man, and on addressing him no response came. "Are you man or the devil?" And still no answer. He was confident it was man; the form and outline gave him the fullest assurance. His next impression was to evade him by turning out of the road and pass by him. Finally summoning up all his courage and relying on his physical strength, (of which he had a good supply,) he approached carefully and then springing, seized a — stump! On seeing the place afterwards, it was revealed to him that a turn in the road and a little opening in the forest beyond, gave the object the appearance of being in the road, and imagination had done the rest.

Another circumstance showing the power of imagination: Horace Thayer made baskets during the winter season, and stored them in all stages of manufacture in a large open chamber. One time he had been away with his wife to spend the evening, and on their return a noise in the chamber indicated the presence of a burglar. The plan of attack was arranged for Mr Thayer to go up stairs, armed with a large club, and his wife to keep guard at the window in case of an escape. But on investigation their fears were removed by finding that the house cat had become a self made prisoner under an overturned basket.

IN OUR GRANDMOTHER'S DAYS.

Written by Mrs. Jerusha King in 1873, at the age of 84, and originally published in the Greenfield Gazzette. It was republished in a Worcester County paper.

I think that you would like to know
How things were done long years ago,
And I have lived to eighty-four
And I can tell what people wore.

Men wore felt hats of coarsest wool,
Boys wore buff caps to church and school,
The ladies they wore pasteboard hats,
Their muffs were made of skins of cats.

Men's clothes were made of wool and flax;
They washed and shaved as neat as wax,
They never looked like Esau's race,
With hair that covered all their face.

The ladies they dressed plain and neat,
In everything from head to feet;
They never wore the thing they call
A *bustle*, or a *waterfall*.

We spun and wove the cloth to wear,
Or worked out in the open air,
We pulled the flax and loaded hay,
And helped to stow it all away.

To card and spin, and knit and sew,
   We learned; all kinds of house-work, too.
To wash and bake, and churn and brew,
   And get up a good dinner, too.

We did not live on pie and cake,
   As 'tis the fashion now;
Our suppers, then, we did not take
   Till we had milked the cow.

And then we had our milk and bread,
Our porridge made of beans, instead;
Or hasty pudding, warm and sweet,
And sometimes we had fish or meat.

Our bread was made of corn and rye,
Bolted, it made our crusts for pie.
We always had enough to eat,
But very seldom any wheat.

We learned to wash and mend our clothes,
   Our stockigns we could darn.
Now, you can't find a girl who knows
   How to spin stocking-yarn.

Then, we worked hard to card and spin
   Our thirty knots a day:
And when the week was done we had
   But fifty cents for pay.

When we had carded, then, and spun
  Our whole nine runs of tow,
'Twould only buy, when it was done,
  One yard of calico.

Of home-spun flax we wove our plaid
  For all our summer wear;
We made it neatly, and were glad
  To wear it anywhere.

We had no school-house, in those times,
  But when the days were warm,
Some one was hired to teach us all
  In father's empty *barn.

And when the time for haying came,
  All worked as they were able.
The barn was filled and school was moved
  Into the clean, dry stable.

You see how hard it must have been
For us to get our learning, then;
But all learned how to read and spell,
And write, too, and we did it well.

We read our Bibles then with care,
Each night we said our evening prayer.
We never were allowed to play
Or work upon God's holy day.

And I am sorry now to say,
That many disregard this day;
This holy day that He has blest—
The emblem of eternal rest.

And thus, in seventy years, or more,
  Great changes have I known;
But of one thing now I'm sure,
  My life is nearly done.

---

*Esther Wood, afterward the wife of Zimri Longley, kept the first school in that part of the town in a barn built by Thomas King, still standing where his son Ezra lived. It was the first framed barn built in town, and was probably built before the incorporation of the town. When it was raised the help was insufficient, and several women rendered assistance.

THE OLD SCHOOLHOUSE.

This was written in 1870. Subject, the old schoolhouse in the old seventh district. Since this was written the old house has been taken down and a new one built. It will vividly portray the youthful experiences of many who have gone forth into the world to struggle with the battles of life.

Erected many years ago by rustic hands,
All faded and worn by the wayside it stands—
With sunburnt, weather beaten walls which knew no paint,
With roof devoid of cornice, and chimney stood aslant,
With solemn looking benches, and blackboard three by four,
With high old fashioned windows, and narrow cleated door.

Such was the theater of my young, ambitious pride,
Sometimes on mischief bent, sometimes for learning tried;
Such was the place where schoolmates met from day to day,
With lessons learned and heard all were intent on play;
Such was the scene of many a grief and joy,
Since first I tried the fortunes of the glad schoolboy.

Since then I've left those once familiar scenes,
And sought 'mong strangers homes to benefit my means;
But those teachers and scholars which I knew of yore,
In my silent thoughts to memory appear,
And when passing, I look with fond regret
At the old school house that stands by the wayside yet.

For those youthful days were the brightest days to me,
So free from busy care, from anxious labor free,
That fain would I return, again to live them o'er,
And pass the pleasant days of school once more;
But, ah! stern duty calls me hence to roam,
And to others I resign my childhood's home.

ORTODOXY VS INFIDELITY.

A contest that was fought out in Franklin County renewed in London.

A singular bit of history is in existence which most of the older people of western Franklin will remember. In the palmy days of the town Dr. Charles Knowlton from Ashburnham settled in Hawley and commenced the practice of his profession. His fame as an advocate of materialism and other views tending to atheism had preceded him, and the staid old orthodox town of Hawley was much excited, especially when it was known that he proposed to publish another edition of his "Fruits of Philosophy," for issuing which he had been imprisoned at Cambridge. A rivalry instantly sprang up between Dr. Knowlton and Dr. Moses Smith, the orthodox physician who had long practiced in the town. Each doctor had his strong partisan friends, and quite a number of families named their children after their favorite physician. Col. Charles Knowlton Hawkes, who recently died in San Francisco, Cal., and Col. Moses Smith Hall of West Virginia, who distinguished himself during the war as colonel of the Virginia regiment which did such efficient service in bushwhack fighting with West Virginia rebels, were both natives of Hawley and were named after Drs. Knowlton and Smith.

Rev. Jonathan Grout, the first settled minister in Hawley, was then living and visited Dr. Knowlton and tried to persuade him to abandon the publication of his book, urging among other reasons, that it was against the law to publish such a book. The doctor replied that he "didn't care anything about the law." Mr. Grout told him that laws were made for people who didn't care anything about them.

About this time Rev. Tyler Thatcher settled in Hawley as colleague with Mr. Grout. He was a young man of rare talent, with reasoning powers of a high order, an argumentative mind, and ultra-Calvinistic views in theology. A brisk controversy immediately sprang up between him and Dr. Knowlton, which resulted in a challenge from Mr Thatcher to the doctor to meet him in a public debate in the old meeting house. The challenge was accepted, the parties met and a great forensic battle was fought between the theism of the Puritan fathers and modern materialism, Dr. Knowlton taking his turn in occupying the pulpit in the old church, from which, up to that day, nothing had emanated but the pure unadulterated theism of the pilgrim fathers. Mr. Thatcher was assisted by a man named Batchelder, who made it his business to travel the country and hold public meetings with infidels. A large audience gathered from the surrounding towns to hear the debate, and the result was the friends of both sides claimed the victory.

About this time Dr. Knowlton removed to Ashfield and formed a copartnership with Dr. Roswell Shepard, and Shepard & Knowlton published the book, the republication of which has raised such an excitement in England. The town of Ashfield was at once divided into two parties, the Knowlton and anti-Knowlton. The Knowlton party was composed, not so much of proselytes of Dr. Knowlton's peculiar notions on materialism, as of persons who had faith in him as being a skillful physician, and who believed it would be better to let him alone, and allow him to peaceably enjoy his own opinions, as up to this time he had made no attempt to make proselytes to his views on materialism. Rev. Mr. Grosvenor, the Congregational minister, made an attack on him from his pulpit, in which he told his people not to employ Shepard & Knowlton,—that infidelity must be crushed in Ashfield by withdrawing patronage from that firm,— and it was proposed to put the ban of the church upon all of its members who persisted in employing them. Dr. Knowlton attended the church meeting and asked permission to speak, but as he was not a church member, that privilege was not granted him. He then published his famous "Letter to Col. Abel Williams," a prominent member of the church who refused to withdraw his patronage from him, in which he maintained his right to disseminate his own opinions, if in doing so he did not infringe upon the rights of others. He called a meeting of the citizens of Ashfield, at which he made a long address, ending by proclaiming his purpose to stick at all hazards, and support himself and family by the practice of his profession in that town.

Immediately after this Rev. Mr. Grosvenor and several of his leading church members appeared before the grand jury at Greenfield, and procured the indictment of Shepard & Knowlton for publishing a book calculated to injure the public morals. This indictment, which was found at the August term in 1834, is a curiously worded document, but, in its phraseology, somewhat similar to one found in England in June, 1877, and tried before the lord justice and a special jury. Knowlton & Shepard were arrested by Sheriffs Purple and Wells, and gave bail for their appearance at the November term, when the case was tried, with District Attorney Dewey for the Commonwealth, and Wells and Alvord for the defendants. The jury disagreed, and the case was re-tried in March, 1835, when the jury again disagreed, and the case was nolprossed at the next (August) term.

It is a curious fact that nothing more is heard of this book for forty three years, till its republication in England caused so much excitement. It is also a remarkable confirmation of Dr. Knowlton's claim to originality in the discovery of certain physiological truths put forth in this book, that it was stated in the English court that after a diligent search through all medical or quasimedical literature, nothing containing similar statements could be found. Mr. Bradlaugh and Mrs. Besant conducted their own defense, the latter occupying several hours in her plea, in which she discussed from a moral and philanthropic standpoint the propriety of scientific checks upon the increase of population. After a three days' trial, the lord chief justice charged the jury that if, in their opinion, the book was calculated to injure the public morals, they were bound to render a verdict of guilty, whether it was published with a bad intent or not. They rendered a verdict of guilty, but exonerated the defendants from any bad motive in publishing the book. Sentence was suspended for a time, and the defendants were released on their own recognizances. Meanwhile a writ of error has been granted, and it is thought the verdict will not be sustained.

BIOGRAPHICAL SKETCHES.

Justin Bliss Warriner, oldest son of Hezekiah Warriner, was born in Hawley, March 15, 1818, and married Laura Alfreda, daughter of Samuel T. Grout. He graduated at the Pennsylvania Medical College and commenced the practice of medicine in Burlington, N. J., in 1848. He died of Asiatic cholera the following year, after having had the remarkable success of not losing a patient from the fell disease, although he treated on an average forty cases a day. People living in that part of Burlington called Beverly still remember the panic his death occasioned, as they had such confidence in his skill that even cholera had lost its terrors.

Hezekiah Ryland Warriner, born in Hawley, July 23, 1822, was educated at Williston Seminary in Easthampton. He spent several years in Deerfield, Greenfield, and surrounding towns, then went to Philadelphia, establishing a brilliant reputation as an educator. He afterwards commenced the study of Law in the office of Henry T. Grout, of Philadelphia, was admitted to the bar, and at the time of his death, which occurred Jan. 31, 1873, in the prime of life, was rapidly rising in his profession. His body was brought to Deerfield for burial, at his request, and his former pupils in the Academy erected a monument to his memory, and by his side rests the body of his beloved wife, Olive, daughter of Capt. Edmund Longley.

Dr. Henry Augustus Warriner, youngest son of Hezekiah Warriner, was born in Hawley, Sept. 21, 1824, graduated from the Medical College in Cincinnati, Ohio, and afterwards spent a year studying in Germany, and then returned to fill a Professorship in Antioch College, Ohio. At the breaking out of the War of the Rebellion he with other teachers and many students enlisted in the union army, and he was assigned the charge of the Western division of Sanitary stores. After the war he spent some years in literary work, mostly in Deerfield, and represented that district in the legislature. He left Deerfield to engage in teaching at Plymouth, where he died suddenly, in November, 1871, in the midst of his usefulness, like his elder brothers.

Henry Taylor Grout, L. L. D., youngest son of Rev. Jonathan Grout, was born in Hawley, Aug. 7, 1810, finished his education at Hamilton, N. Y. He at first engaged in mercantile business at Grafton, Mass., where he was postmaster until he left the place. He finally located in

Philadelphia and commenced the study of law in the office of Judge Kelly, and was in partnership with him for some years after being admitted to the bar. He was a staunch Democrat, and at one time when the city was largely democratic he was strongly urged to accept the nomination for Mayor of the city, but he declined, preferring to continue in the practice of his profession. For several years he was City Solicitor for the District of Pennsylvania. He died June 22, 1886.

The ancestry of the Longleys who settled in Hawley is traced back 220 years to William Longley, who was town clerk of Groton in 1666. His son William was also town clerk, and with his family was massacred by Indians, July 27, 1694.

Edmund Longley was a prominent, influential man, was a Justice of the Peace, the first town clerk, serving thirteen consecutive years, and for thirteen terms represented his town in the legislature. He was a natural leader among his cotemporaries, and many of his descendants inherit the same quality. He possessed a good business ability and was polished and gentlemanly. He was a colonel in the Revolutionary war, and in after life received a pension of $296 a year. He died Nov. 29, 1842, at the advanced age of 96 years. Of his children, none are living, and of his descendants but one family remains in Hawley, that of Mrs. Edwin Scott, a great granddaughter.

Gen. Thomas Longley, oldest son of "Esq. Edmund," was born Sept. 4, 1774. Like his father, he was prominent and influential, for many years was town clerk, and was many times sent to the legislature. He was undoubtedly the ablest man of his time who represented the town in the General Court, was a fine public speaker, carrying a strong and positive influence, and was possessed of much dignity and bearing. Unlike most country members of the present day, his voice could be heard with telling effect in the halls of legislation, and in his day he was one of the most widely known and esteemed men in this part of the state. During the war of 1812 he was placed in command of a regiment of infantry drafted from the northern part of the old County of Hampshire, (now Franklin County,) with orders to march to Boston to protect the coast from invasion. He settled with his father, outliving him but six years, and died at Hawley, Sept. 22, 1848.

Alfred Longley, son of Thomas, born at Hawley, Nov. 10, 1809, graduated from Oberlin College, Ohio, studied theology with Dr. Packard of Shelburne, and was licensed to preach by the Franklin Association. He afterwards preached in northern Ohio, and died at Chatham Centre, in that state, in 1850, aged 41.

Thomas Lawrence Longley, son of Thomas, was born in Hawley, Feb. 15, 1821. At the age of 22 he went to Dakota to assist his brother and sister, Mr. and Mrs. Riggs, in establishing themselves at a new missionary station. Soon after reaching there he was drowned while bathing in the river. This sudden ending of a life of so much promise was not only a dreadful blow to his sister and her family, but also to his old father and mother at home, as they had hoped he would soon return to cheer their declining years. It was also a great loss to the town, as no more worthy son ever left the hills of old Hawley. His parting injunction to a cousin to "do good and be good" had been his own motto, as his beautiful, unselfish life abundantly proved.

Joseph G. Longley, youngest son of Thomas, was born in Hawley, May 24, 1843. After his common school life at home he became a student at Oberlin, Ohio, came home on a visit, and remained on account of his fathers' poor health. After teaching some years, a part of which time he served as a member of the School Committee in his native town, he enlisted in the army, and was 1st lieutenant in the 1st Massachusetts colored regiment. His health failing, he was discharged, and was employed by the American Missionary Association, as Superintendent of schools among the Freedmen of North Carolina. He afterwards graduated from the Theological Seminary at Auburn, N. Y., and soon after died at Greenville, Ill., May 4, 1871. aged nearly 48.

Mrs. Lucretia Longley Cooley, daughter of Thomas Longley, was born at Hawley, Oct. 4, 1811, and died at Marysville, C.l. in 1881, where she had resided with her sons seven years, after the death of her husband, in South Deerfield.

Mary Ann Longley, daughter of Thomas, born March 10, 1813, married Rev. Stephen R. Riggs in 1837, and started for the land of the Dakotas, where her life for the next thirty two years was spent in assisting her husband in his efforts to civilize and christianize the natives, and in caring for and educating her own family of eight children. Those who have read "Mary and I," written by her husband after her death, will have no doubt that the plaudit "Well done" awaited her in "Jerusalem the Golden." She died March 22, 1869, aged 55.

One of their sons visited the east last autumn, lecturing in the interests of the cause in which his parents were engaged. During his travels he visited Hawley.

Henrietta Arms Longley, youngest daughter of General Longley, was born July 12, 1826, was educated at South Hadley Seminary, taught at Mauch Chunk, Pa., died in 1850, at the age of 24.

The following is copied from an issue of the Greenfield Gazette in June, 1882:—

Mrs. Jerusha King, who died in Plainfield, May 29, was a representative of one of the oldest families in Hawley. Her grandfather, Thomas King, came into town in the spring of 1772, the second year of its settlement. She was a direct descendant on her maternal side of Gain Robinson, a clergyman who emigrated from Scotland in 1682, being his great granddaughter. (The writer is a descendant of the same stock.) The subject of this sketch was born in Hawley, Nov. 25, 1788, which was three years before the town was incorporated and received its name, and was therefore 93 years old at the time of her death. At the age of 18 she married Ezra King, thereby not changing her maiden name, and became the mother of 15 children, seven of whom survive her, the oldest at the age of 75. She has been almost a life-long resident of her native town, and in the same neighborhood of her birth, having lived at one place forty years. She was possessed of a fine physical constitution, was active and industrious, and for many long years "Aunt" Jerusha's hospitality was extended to friends, relatives and strangers. Her name was a household word and she was one of those town aunts who is a friend to every body. About forty years ago her husband died, and about twenty five years ago she went to live with her brother and manage his household, he being a widower, and remained until his death in 1877. Mr. King died with that terrible scourge, a cancer, which ate away the entire side of his face, and his sister, then 88 years of age, had the whole care of him, being obliged to get up several times each night for a number of months, and without shrinking and with Christian fortitude did she minister at that bedside until death relieved him of his sufferings. She then went to live with her daughter, Mrs. Jones, in Plainfield, where she quietly passed the last five years of her life, surrounded by the love of all who knew her. And now, after her life work is done, and nobly done, having rounded up almost a century, this venerable mother in Israel peacefully sleeps in the cemetey in Hawley, and her children, all of whom occupy respectable positions in life, rise up and call her blessed.

Warriner King was born in Hawley, May 27, 1787. On arriving at his majority he married Elizabeth Crowell and bought a farm adjoining his birthplace, which is the present town farm, which he greatly improved by erecting substantial buildings, enclosing the fields with stone walls, and clearing up the original forest. He operated a sawmill and turning shop for many years, and done some local business at making and mending shoes. He lived without ostentation, but possessed a sound, matured judgment, receiving the highest offices in the gift of the town. It was a motto with him "What is worth doing is worth doing well." In his religious sentiments he was a Methodist, and in the old days of circuit preachers his hospitality was shared by many of those itinerants.

His voice in prayer, exhortation and song was often heard in the conference meeting. After becoming disabled from age and infirmity he sold his farm and bought a homestead near by, where he spent the rest of his days, enjoying a competency which his hands earned in the prime of life. He died Feb. 27, 1877, at the age of almost 90, having passed his entire life within half a mile of his birthplace.

Jonas King, son of Jonas and Abigail (Leonard) King, was born in Hawley, July 29, 1792. His parents were poor, and the avenues for obtaining an education were limited in those primitive days, but he had a strong desire for learning and used every means in his power in that pursuit. In his boyhood he once went to a schoolhouse in Plainfield, where he knew there was a school, arriving the first one on the ground in the morning. When the master came he asked him who he was and what he wanted. On learning his history, the master took him into the school and afterwards made arrangements to give him the benefit of that term. His schooldays were but a succession of stuggles for the object in view, but he fitted for college, and graduated at Williams in 1816, at the age of 22, studied theology at Andover, and was ordained in 1819. In 1823 he went with Pliny Fisk as a missionary to Jerusalem, and in 1828 became a missionary to Greece, where he labered the remainder of his life, being an able and efficient power in behalf of the oppressed inhabitants. In 1865 he made his last visit to America, at which time he preached once in his native town, and was the object of marked attention elsewhere in this country. He died in Greece since his return.

George Lathrop, son of Zephaniah, was born in Hawley, March 5, 1795. Able and public spirited, he was identified with the interests of the town, held the office of town clerk, and selectman, and was several times sent as a Representative to the legislature. The material for the history of Hawley in Dr. Holland's "History of Western Massachusetts" published in 1855, was furnished in part by him. Honest and conscientious, he was upright in all his dealings. He died Sept. 8, 1862.

Rufus Sears, when a boy of 11 years, came ftom Dennis with Joseph Bangs, and lived to advanced age in Hawley, At different periods he served as deacon of both the churches in town, had a strongly marked religious character, and held the respect of all who knew him. During the last of his life he used to stand in the pulpit beside the minister, during services, on account of deafness. He lived to see the burial of his namesake, a grandson who had grown to manhood. His death occurred Nov. 6, 1856.

Freeman Atkins, born in Coleraine, Aug. 21, 1806, spent the most of his life in Hawley, where Zenas Baugs settled in Pudding Hollow. Has served as town clerk and on the board of selectmen, and for thirty-seven years was Treasurer of the Congregational society in West Hawley, the duties of which he ever discharged with promptness and fidelity. He was a large, well proportioned man, and in his prime but few had a finer physical development. It was a characteristic of his to do his work in the neatest manner, and everything coming under his supervision was marked with the most perfect order. The neat, substantial farm buildings which he erected, and his principles of strict integrity and sobriety are a sufficient monument to his memory. He died Nov. 30, 1879.

Lyman F. Griggs was born in Hawley, Oct. 19, 1821, but went away in early life to shift for himself. He applied himself to studying and teaching for some time, when he turned his attention to the study of medicine, went to a Medical college in Philadelphia, where he graduated and located for practice at Ware, Mass., giving promise of a bright future, but died soon after. His wife was a Miss Powers of Brimfield.

Clark Sears, born in Ashfield, Jan. 30, 1804, passed the majority of his life in Hawley, and died Nov. 29, 1879. He represented both his town and district in the legislature, and was often moderator of the town meetings. "Uncle Clark" was a plain-spoken, good-hearted man, and was in every way worthy of confidence and esteem.

Henry Martyn Seymour was a young man of promise, was a son of Rev. Henry Seymour, was for several years connected with the Springfield Union. He died suddenly in 1876, in Hadley, where he had gone with his bride of a month to keep Thanksgiving. His age was 28.

Horace Dwight Seymour, another son of Rev. Henry Seymour, was associated with his brother in business in Brooklyn, N. Y., and was also a brilliant and promising young man. Being ill, he came home to Hawley to recuperate, but sank under the disease, and died March 19, 1886, aged 24 years.

Dennis W. Baker was born in Hawley, Jan. 16, 1829, and married Lucretia Vincent. He was an able, efficient business man, for a term of years was a manufacturer of broomhandles, and for the last eight years he remained in Hawley, was town clerk, was also a prominent member of the church choir. He afterwards removed to Charlemont, where he operated a lumber mill. For a time he was Treasurer of the Deerfield Valley Agricultural Society, the duties of which he performed ably and promptly. He also served on the board of selectmen of Charlemont, and died in that town in the midst of his usefulness.

BOZRAH.

CONTRIBUTED BY GEO. D. CRITTENDEN OF SHELBURNE FALLS, FOR THIS WORK.

This neighborhood, which is in the north part of the town, a mile and a half south of Charlemont village, was settled in 1775, by five families from Bozrah, Ct., a small town which was formerly a part of Norwich.

The heads of four of these families were Zebedee Wood, Joseph Edgerton, Zephaniah Lathrop and Gershom West. The name of the fifth family is not known to the writer.

Zebedee Wood seems to have been the pioneer, as he came to spy out the land in May, 1774. A diary which he kept during his journey shows that he was gone about twenty-three days, and his travelling expenses were 17 shillings, six pence and 2 farthings, or about $4 25, and the distance covered by the round trip was 243 miles. He was a farmer, tanner and shoemaker, and his wife was a tailoress. She was also for several years the only person in town who acted as a physician. On one occasion her services were wanted in a family at Pudding Hollow, some two miles distant. The snow was very deep, there was no road, and travelling was impracticable. A spruce tree was cut, the top cut off, on which she was drawn by several men, and rendered the necessary aid. Mr. Wood settled on the place now occupied by Frank Simpson, and built a log house and a small tannery a short distance west of where Mr. Simpson now lives. In the summer of 1785 he built the house now occupied by Mr. Simpson, which is supposed to be the oldest house now occupied in town. His barn was built in 1784. He was for several years clerk of No. 7, the name by which the town was called before its incorporation. He was one of the minute men who responded to the call of Gen. Stark, and assisted in defeating Col. Baum at the battle of Bennington, on the 16th of August, 1777.

Zephaniah Lathrop, who settled on the place now occupied by W. E. Mansfield, was for many years a prominent man, both as a town official and an officer in the church.

Gershom West, who settled where Mr. Clemons now lives, is supposed to have kept the first retail store in town.

Joseph Edgerton settled on the farm recently occupied by the late Erastus Brayman. His son Ezekiel succeeded him on the homestead, and besides being a farmer, he was a master mechanic. There were but few houses, churches or mills built in that vicinity for many years that were not under his supervision.

A native of the neighborhood, who has long been abroad, gives the location of the families there about 1820:—

"On the hill, south, was Eben Maynard and his mother; at the foot of the hill, Ethan Hitchcock, next, widow Taylor, Ichabod Hawkes, Abisha Rogers, Elisha Sanford, Samuel Wing, Andrew Wood, Simeon Crittenden, Zephaniah Lathrop, Ezekiel Edgerton; at the foot of the hill, north, Isaac Packard; commencing east, Capt. Ellis, Noah Look, Oliver Edgerton, Levi Leonard; in the "Turkey pen," Seth Salisbury; next, Oliver Patch, Abel Parker. Mr. Parker succeeded Mr. Patch in the clothier business. A man whose name I cannot recall, once lived on the Samuel Wing farm and accidentally killed his wife by falling a tree on her.

The following family history is from a member of the Edgerton family, and a native of the town:—

Capt. Joseph Edgerton came from England,— in what year is not known,— and settled in Norwich, Ct. He was lost at sea and his ship never heard of. When he came to Norwich he brought with him four sons and one daughter, whose names were Simeon, Benjamin, William, Joseph and Hannah. Hannah married a man by the name of Lefenwell, and settled in Salisbury, Ct., Simeon settled in Pawlet, Vt., Benjamin settled in Bennington, Vt., William settled in Hartford, Ct., and was a seafaring man.

Joseph Edgerton, the youngest son, was born in 1738, married Lucy Lyon and came with his family of six children to Hawley in 1775, being literally one of the fathers of the town. Their children's names were Darius, Oliver, Joseph, Ezekiel, Asa, Nancy, and Lucy, who was born in Hawley. He died in 1809, and his wife in 1823, and at the time of her death her descendants numbered 58.

Darius married Mary Beckwith, and had five children, Eunice, Betsey Amy, Maria, and one died in infancy. He settled in Charlemont, and from there removed to Ovid, N. Y., where he died in 1840. All his children have been dead some years.

Oliver married Persis Rice, having no children, and settled on the place now owned by Charles Crittenden, when the land was in a wilderness state. He removed to Brecksville, Ohio, in 1831, where he died in 1849. His wife died in 1836.

Joseph married Candace Rice and they had eleven children, all born in Hawley, viz:— Dexter, Saphronia, Oliver, Joseph, Elias, Wells, Orie, Austin, Candace and Ruth. The two oldest are buried in the cemetery in Bozrah. He removed with his family to Brecksville, Ohio, in 1815, being one of the first settlers of that town, then a wilderness. He died in 1842, his wife in in 1855, and the last of their children died in 1886. All but two died in Brecksville, one in Missouri and one in Wisconsin. They were all farmers.

Ezekiel Edgerton succeeded to the homestead, and was the only one of his name and generation whose life was spent and family reared in Hawley. He was a farmer and mechanic, and besides being a carpenter and builder he had a shop in which he made various kinds of cabinet work, wagons and sleighs. He was a very well educated man of his day. He married Lucy, daughter of Dea. Ebenezer Fales of Charlemont, in 1800. They had twelve children, as follows: Harvey, born in 1801, Almira, born in 1803, John, born in 1805, Justus, born 1806, Sardis, born in 1808, Ann, born in 1809, David, born in 1811, Eliza, born in 1813, Clarinda, born in 1815, (the writer of this sketch,) Ezekiel, born in 1817 Lucy F., born in 1818, Hiram B., born in 1820. The father died in 1837, the mother in 1823, are buried in the cemetery in Bozrah, and by their side rests three of their children, Eliza, whose death occurred the same year of her mother's, Lucy and Ezekiel. Three of them died in North Royalton, Ohio, Hiram in 1884, aged 64, John in 1883, aged 79, David in 1837, aged 26. Harvey is living at No. Royalton, O., aged 86, Justus is living at Brecksville, O., aged 81, Sardis is living at Royalton, aged 79, Clarinda is living at Brecksville, aged 72.

Asa married Lydia Washburn and settled in the west part of the town. They had eight children; Laura and Electa died in childhood, Aurelia, Miranda, Lydia, Sarah, Samuel lives in Palmer, runs an iron foundry, Mary Ann, lives in Cleveland, O. From Hawley he removed to Oneida Co., N. Y., where he died soon after.

Nancy married Leonard White, and settled in Coleraine, and had seven children, Amasa, Anson, Ezekiel, Othniel, Zilpha, Lucy and Saphrona. None of them are living but Othniel.

Lucy married Alfred Rice; their children were Alonzo, Lorenzo, is a manufacturer in Washington, D. C., Sybil, Abigail, Huldah, Quartus, a merchant in Pueblo, Col., and Chloe. Mr. Rice was a mechanic; he died in Savoy many years ago, his wife in North Adams.

Prices that ruled in Hawley one hundred years ago.

Potatoes, per bushel,	1 shilling	Shoes, per pair,	6 shillings
Wheat, per bushel,	4 shillings	Labor, per day,	2 shillings
Rye, per bushel,	3 shillings	Labor, man and team,	6 shillings
Corn, per bushel,	3 shillings	Salt, per bushel,	5 shillings 6d
Beans, per bushel,	4 shillings	Butter, per lb.,	6d
Oats, per bushel,	18d	Hayseed, per lb.,	1 shilling 1d
Tobacco, per lb.,	6d	Rum, per gal.,	4 shillings
Candles, per lb.,	9d	Oil, per gal.,	7 shillings
Salt pork, per lb.,	6d	Sugar, per lb.,	6d
Mutton, per lb.,	2d	Wool, per lb.,	18d
Beef, per lb.,	4d 2 far	Tea, per lb.,	4 shillings
Swine, live weight, per lb,	2d	Making coat,	3 shillings
Veal, per lb,	2d	Making shoes, per pair,	1s 8d

Note. It is probable that a shilling of that currency was about 24 cents.

NATIVES ABROAD.

Rev. Moses M. Longley was born in Hawley, June 14, 1814. He graduated from the Seminary and College at Oberlin, Ohio, and preached in that state till 1855, when he returned to Massachusetts and located in Peru, representing that town once in the legislature in 1866, afterwards preached in Washington and in Fitchburg. In 1869 he removed to Illinois, and was a settled pastor at Dwights and Danvers. Since 1883 he has been employed by the Illinois Home Missionary Society, in preaching for feeble churches and organizing new ones. He is now living at Bloomington, Ill.

Abner T. Longley was for twenty years, until the present administration came into power, one of the chief officers in the Agricultural Department at Washington. His wife, —Abigail King,— is also a native of the town.

Henry A. Longley left Hawley in 1836, and resides in Northampton. Some of his early life was spent in teaching, and for nearly thirty years he was Sheriff of Hampshire County, the first term by appointment, the other terms by election, and was always a popular official.

Chalmers P. Longley is a musical composer in Boston.

Elijah F. Longley is a farmer in Charlemont.

Roswell Eldridge resides in Charlemont, his wife being a daughter of Capt. Edmund Longley.

Flora A. Longley, wife of Nathaniel Lampson resides at Shelburne Falls.

Mrs. Abigail (King) Barton is living at Plainfield, aged nearly 87. She is the last representative of the third generation from Thomas King, remaining in New England.

Mrs. Roana (King) Bangs, widow of Dennis Bangs is living at Hamilton, N. Y., at the age of 89.

Mrs. Mercy (King) Rice resides at North Adams. Her son has recently been appointed postmaster in that town.

Mrs. Chloe (King) Jones has lived for a long term of years in Plainfield, and now lives at Oshkosh, Wisconsin.

Mrs. Olive B. (King) Coope is living at Shelburne Falls.

Mrs. Jerusha (King) Joy resides at Shelburne Falls.

Mariette Baker, wife of Charles B. Mayhew, resides at Charlemont.

Preston Baker is an extensive dealer in flour and grain at Charlemont.

Edwin Baker resides at Shelburne Falls. He has represented his district two terms in the legislature, is a druggist, and enjoys a large degree of confidence and esteem in business and social circles.

Mrs. Ereda (Baker) Buddington resides in Leyden.

Allen C. Baker was formerly a farmer in East Charlemont, but now lives somewhere at the west.

Timothy Baker formerly lived in Savoy, was sent from there one term to the legislature, now lives in Adams, has been a coal dealer.

Nathan B. Baker is a farmer in Savoy. He is quite prominent among his townsmen in agricultural and political circles.

Clark W. Fuller has been a lumber dealer, merchant, hotel keeper and farmer, and now keeps a large boarding house at 5 & 7, Northfield street, Boston.

Albert E. Marsh is living at Northampton. His wife, Anna, was a daughter of Wells and Bathsheba Ayres, of Hawley.

Theodore C. Marsh is living at Whitingham, Vt.

Abraham Parker 3d resides at Amherst.

Joseph Marsh is a bookseller and newsdealer, and prominent citizen of Northampton.

Jonathan Marsh, brother of Joseph, lives in Corry, Pa.

Loron Marsh, brother of Joseph, resides at Riceville, Pa.

Theophilus Crosby is a business man in Manchester, Iowa. His golden wedding was celebrated Oct. 26, 1886.

Clark R. Griggs has probably been the most successful business man originating from Hawley. He was born March 6, 1824; at the age of 8 years he went to live with his uncle Waldo Griggs at Brimfield. He obtained a good education but was not a college graduate, and preached a term of years at Westboro, for the Adventists. During the war he was post sutler at Memphis, Tenn., being appointed by the government. Since then he has been a railroad contractor, and has built several roads. He is ranked among the millionares, and has an office in New York city. His residence cost $75,000.

Andrew J. Griggs learned the trade of making matches at the shop of H. E. Pierce in Charlemont, afterwards conducting the business in Williamsburg and at Pittsburg, Pa. He is now in Chicago, Ill., and is a large real estate owner and broker.

Charles R. Griggs is a shoe manufacturer in Westboro, has been successful in business, and is probably worth $100,000.

Newell Hunt, oldest son of Elisha and Louisa M. Hunt, went to Memphis, Tenn., in 1863, at the age of 20, in the employ of his uncle, Clark R. Griggs, and remained with him until the close of the war. Then with his brother, Lyman G., he engaged in the manufacture of matches in Chicago, Ill., where he remained until the great fire of 1871, when their factory was burned. For the last fifteen years he has been engaged at dairying, first at Kenosha, Wis., now at Diamond Lake, Ill., having the milk of 300 cows, or 10,000 pounds a day to make into butter and cheese.

Lyman G. Hunt is in Leadville, Col, has an office at 524 Elm St. The following is clipped from a late copy of the Leadville Chronicle:—

"There is no one to-day who commands a more enviable identity with the career of this young giant metropolis than Mr. L. G. Hunt, the pioneer scale man, whose handiwork is visible upon every thoroughfare in the city, and whose name embodies all the attributes that are noble. His business operations have always been stamped with honesty, and no transaction has gone without the broad seal of integrity. Coming here from the east in an early day and deciding to trust his destiny upon the waves that were then rocking the city and tossing its future from side to side, Mr. Hunt engaged in the scale business, being the authorized representative of the famous Fairbanks scales company of Chicago. · · · · · ·
In supplying the miner with the facilities for the correct weighing of his output, Mr. Hunt has erected a large number of these scales at the mines and in the city, while a large number of orders were filled during last year. At his works on Elm street, may be seen every size and pattern of their invention of scales, and business men who find it to their interest to guard, carefully, the welfare of their patrons, will do well to visit Mr. Hunt before supplying their houses with permanent and reliable fixtures. The gentleman also repairs and adjusts scales, and gives prompt attention to all orders."

Ellen J. Hunt is the wife of Dr. Josiah Trow, resides in Buckland.

Flora L. Hunt married C. A. Bronson, and resides in Ashfield.

Josiah H. Hunt was born Dec. 26, 1835. He attended the common schools in his native town, went to Kimball Union Academy, at Meriden, N. H., and graduated at Amherst College. He taught three terms each year for twenty-one consecutive years, the most of that time in Clinton and Gloucester, in this state, and finding the confinement too severe for his health, and a change necessary, he relinquished teaching, and established himself in Topeka, Kansas, as a real estate broker. He is conducting a large and successful business, in the interests of which he annually makes two trips to the east.

Henry F. Sears is a graduate of Amherst, and a successful teacher in Boston. His residence is at Somerville.

Freeman B. Sears is at the west, and has been identified with the sewing machine interest.

Lewis E. Sears is a farmer in Plainfield.

Clara B. (Sears) Childs resides in Deerfield, wife of Theodore Childs.

Merrick J. Holden is doing a large business as lumber dealer in Adams. His wife is a daughter of Nathan Mason of Hawley.

Charles N. Holden is a farmer in Plainfield.

Eliza (Holden) Stockwell is the wife of Hosea W. Stockwell of Plainfield.

Henry Howes resides in Cheshire. Himself and wife and children, some of whom remain with their parents, are all natives of Hawley. Lovina is living at Northampton, Wealthy is living in Ohio.

Morris Vincent is a farmer at Milan, Mich.

Albert Vincent is living at Sterling, Ill, is a travelling salesman for agricultural tools.

Thomas M. Carter resides at Williamsburg, is a druggist. He is town clerk, a Justice of the Peace, has been one of the selectmen several years, and in every way enjoys the confidence and esteem of his townsmen. His wife is also a native of the town, being a daughter of the late John Vincent, Esq.

Samuel Taylor Grout, son of Rev. Jonathan Grout, at the age of 83, is living at Deerfield with his three daughters, Laura Alfreda, Mary P. and Lucy E., all pleasantly located in that old historic town.

Samuel Dorr Lascombe is a business man in Milwaukie, Wis., lives in fine style on one of the principal avenues of the city, and is taxed for $100,000

Julia A. Rice, daughter of Sylvanus, is married and lives in Buckland.

Mary F., another daughter, is the wife of Daniel Ingraham and lives in Savoy.

Newell S. Rice is a farmer in Ohio. He served in the army during the entire term of the War of the Rebellion, and made an honorable record.

Roswell G. Rice, son of Champion B., is a tinner in Conway.

Calvin E. Cooley, and wife, and children, are natives of Hawley, now residents of Charlemont. Mr Cooley is a prosperous farmer.

Moses M. Mantor is a farmer in Charlemont. For several years he has been the able and efficient Secretary of the Deerfield Valley Agricultural Society. His wife is a daughter of the late Dea. Samuel Hall.

Fidelia T. (Mantor) Howes has lived in Ashfield since her marriage.

Mrs Martha (Taylor) Hamlin is the wife of Dea. Freeman Hamlin of Plainfield.

William C. Ford has for many years been a resident of Fairhaven, Ms.

Mrs. Mary (Ford) Bradford has resided in Conway since her marriage, about fifty-five years.

Harriet S. Harmon, daughter of Levi Harmon, married Joshua T. Davis and resides in Buckland.

Ellen J. (Harmon) Ward resides in Buckland.

Rev. Elijah Harmon is living in Wilmington, Mass., served in the army, graduate of Amherst, in 1861, formerly preached at Winchester, N. H.

Joseph V. Harmon is living at Florence.

Six of the sons of Jonathan Damon are in business in the state of Connecticut; Homer F. in New Britain, Henry C. in Meriden.

Dwight Smith has a position in a bank in Pittsfield.

Joseph Smith is a tradesman in Pittsfield.

Elisha Clark is a farmer in Illinois.

Samuel Clark resides in Williamsburg.

Dwight E. Sanford is an attendant at the Retreat for the Insane, at Hartford, Ct. His brother William J. also lives at Hartford.

Wesley Beals and William H. Beals are living in Plainfield.

Lorenzo W. Joy is a resident of Northampton, and for a long term of years was postmaster in that town, and was removed by the present administration from purely partisan principles.

Nelson and Henry Joy formerly kept a boarding house in Washington, D. C. Among their patrons were Senator Wilson, one year, Senator Dawes six years, and several Congressmen. Their brother-in-law, Hiram King, was connected with them in the hotel and boarding house business, also owned a hotel at that fashionable resort, Saratoga, and another brother-in-law, Abner T. Longley, held a government office at the same time. Nelson was messenger at the U. S. Capitol for thirteen years, and for eleven years Henry was connected with the government book-bindery. They now occupy a fine residence together at Shelburne Falls, having retired from business.

Ashbel W. Carter is a retired resident of Shelburne Falls, has a house adjoining that of his brothers in-law, the Joys.

Phineas S. Carter went west in early life, has been a farmer, and has recently been connected with a sheep ranch in Kansas.

Capt. Ebenezer Maynard is enjoying a green old age at Shelburne Falls. He was for many years in the mercantile business in that place and at Buckland, has been connected with banking and other business.

Ellen R. Carter is the wife of Amos L. Avery, a wealthy merchant of Charlemont.

Sylvia C. Carter married Thomas Mayhew, and resides at Shelburne Falls.

Maria Carter married Kendrick T. Slate and resides in Greenfield.

Charles Dodge is a lawyer at Toledo, Ohio.

Of the three children of Noah Ford, born in Hawley, John Wesley is a wealthy farmer in Stockbridge, Hester A. married Francis F. Briggs, and lives in Windsor, Elisha W. is a farmer and teacher in Kansas.

Dr. David T. Vining has been for many years a physician in Conway.

Martha A. Doane was a teacher in her native town in early life, and removed to Ohio, thence to Michigan, married Geo. Jourdian. After her husband's death she returned east with her children and now lives in Northampton.

Helen C. Doane married Frank Beals and for many years has resided in Florence.

George W. Doane is a carpenter and builder in Holyoke.

Three of the grandsons of John Taylor, the pioneer, are living; Henry, at Williamsburg, at the age of 83, Daniel, living in Cummington, at the age of 74, and John, living at Savoy.

Daniel Starks went to Ohio in early life, where he has since resided.

Henry Watson Starks has for several years lived at North Adams.

James La Roy Atkins is living in Conway.

Daniel H. Gould is a blacksmith in Plainfield.

Julia Porter Hawkes, daughter of Ichabod, married Richard N. Oakman, Aug. 10, 1841, and resides in Montague. Mr. Oakman is president of the Crocker National Bank.

Richard N. Oakman, Jr. was born in Hawley, Sept. 23, 1843, was educated at Williamstown, now a resident of Greenfield. He is the largest stockholder in, and Treasurer and manager of, the John Russell Cutlery works at Turner's Falls, the largest of the kind in this country, if not in the world.

Thomas K. Wheeler is a farmer in Plainfield. His birthplace is on the same place as that of his illustrious uncle, Jonas King, the missionary.

Julia A. Hawkes, daughter of Levi, is married and lives at Northampton.

James R. Hawkes, son of Levi, is living in Boston.

B. Parsons Mansfield has for many years resided in Easthampton.

George D. Crittenden has for a long time resided at Shelburne Falls. He is an extensive dealer in lumber, making a specialty of white beech timber for planes. He served two terms as one of the Franklin County Commissioners, as a politician is an ardent temperance worker, and has been candidate for representative on the prohibition ticket.

Samuel T. Field is a practicing lawyer at Shelburne Falls. He was once District Attorney for the district including Franklin and Hampshire Counties.

Phineas Loyd Page is a lawyer in Ann Arbor, Mich.

Dr. Charles L. Knowlton is a practicing physician in Northampton.

Pindar Field Cooley resides in Pittsfield, and is a travelling salesman for an Albany house. He has been connected with several branches of mercantile business, having taken his first lesson in the store of the late Calvin S. Longley. He is possessed of a very clever business ability, a pleasing address, and his general "make up" is indicative of the live Yankee.

Thomas K. Baker has been for many years a resident of Springfield.

John H. Larrabee was a Hawley soldier, in the old 10th Mass. Regt., doing efficient service. For many years he has been living at the west.

Nellie, daughter of Henry B. White married Frank E. Mason, and resides in Savoy.

Four of the children of Ezekiel Edgerton are living in Ohio, at advanced ages.

Many others who originated from Hawley are living abroad, whose names have not been obtained. Among the list are probably some of the Longleys, Scotts, Halls, Parkers, Hitchcocks, Holdens, Bakers, Taylors, Dodges and others who were once representative families.

Personal Reminiscences of P. L. Page.

My father, Phineas Page, settled in Hawley with his newly married wife, on the place where he always lived while he resided there, in 1804. There were born to them eight sons and three daughters, all of whom arrived to years of maturity, all were baptized in the old yellow meeting house on the hill, and all were members of the Congregational church.

I remained at home till I was 18, helping my father on his farm, attending the district school in the winter, for about ten weeks each year. This was all the scholastic training I ever had, except a term in the Ashfield Academy, and a short attendance at a high school in Charlemont, and one in Pittsfield, making in all about six months. In Oct. 1837, I left Hawley, and taught school in the state of New York till July, 1838. In the meantime my father's family had removed to Pittsfield, to which place I returned. After teaching school and keeping books in a cotton factory for some time, I turned my attention to the study of the law, in the office of the late Hon. Ensign H. Kellogg, and was admitted to the bar in 1844, and passed the most of my professional life in Pittsfield. I was Judge of the police court there for about twelve years, from 1858 to 1870. In 1838 I united with the first Congregational church there in 1838, and for a number of years was a deacon in the church. In 1842 the late Dr. John Todd became our pastor. In 1849 the South church, including 130 of our number, was formed, with Rev. Samuel Harris of Conway, now Dr. Harris, professor in Yale Theological Seminary, as our first pastor. In 1873, my health having failed, I removed to this place (Ann Arbor, Mich.,) to recuperate and educate my family, where I have since resided.

My brother, Joel S. Page, graduated at Williams in 1846, taught in an academy in Georgia a year and a half, studying law at the same time, returned to Pittsfield, and was admitted to the bar in 1850. He then entered into partnership with myself in the practice of law in Pittsfield, which was continued to 1857, when he removed to Chicago, Ill., where he continued the practice until his death, in 1883.

I had a brother next older than myself, Increase B. Page, who entered Williams College with my brother Joel in the autumn of 1842. In their class were Brewster and Conn, both of whom became foreign missionaries, and now deceased. My brother purposed to enter upon the same work, but he died Aug. 15, 1843, of consumption, at Pittsfield, which was the first death that occurred in our family.

The items in regard to Alvah, a graduate of Amherst, and Theophilus, a graduate of Williams, are familiar. I had also a brother, Horatio F. Page, who graduated from the Berkshire Medical College in 1836. He spent the most of his life in the practice of his profession in Sycamore, Ill., and died there in 1873.

As the years pass on, and I retire from active life, the familiar scenes of my childhood and early youth pass like a panorama before my mind. I seem to be in the old meeting house on the hill, in the old-fashioned square pews, hung on hinges, and turned up for greater ease in standing, at prayer time, seeing the good old deacons, Newton and Sears, under the high pulpit, hearing the powerful voice of good old Parson Grout, in opening the morning devotions, and then adding to the general noise all over the house, in turning down the seats at their conclusion.

But of far greater interest to me was the music of the large choir in the gallery, preceded by a knock of the pitch-pipe by uncle Ethan Hitchcock, and a few strokes on the bass viol by Col. Longley.

I must refer to two old customs which made quite an impression on my youthful mind. Our pastor, Mr. Grout, in making calls among his charge, would talk with each member personally, concerning his or her spiritual condition, and then as he left, standing at the door, would give some words of general exhortation to all. This custom, though sometimes distasteful, making the minister's visits dreaded, especially by the young, was, I think, on the whole, beneficial for those times.

The other custom grew out of the law as it then existed, in proclaiming the bans of matrimony. There were two courses open to a couple entering into this state. They might be "cried" by the town clerk in open assembly. Well do I remember how Gen. Longley, who was always town clerk in those days, would rise just before the minister opened the exercises, and amid profound silence, except a little flutter and giggle among the young people, proclaim in stentorian tones, "Hear ye, hear ye, marriage intended between—and—." Or if the young couple shrank from this oral publicity the bans could be written, and stand for three public days near the church door. The glass box for this purpose, near the front door of the meeting house, was well watched by the young, and often looked into by the elders.

More than half a century since, Gen Thomas Longley was by far the most influential man in Hawley, or any of the surrounding towns, and deservedly so. The last time he represented Hawley in the legislature, and a short time before his death, I happened to be in Boston. I sent in my name to him in the House of Representatives, and he immediately came to the door and invited me to a seat near him. It was not long before he rose and made one of his characteric speeches, condensed, strongly delivered and effective. The Pittsfield representative told me that he was one of the most influential members of the House.

At the meeting of the A. B. C. F. M., held in Pittsfield in 1866, Jonas King, then on a visit from Greece, delivered an address at the South church. At its conclusion, I introduced myself to him as from Hawley, giving my name, which at first he hardly seemed to recognize. I told him I understood that my father hired him to teach his first district school, when a young man. He then said, "Ah! yes, many a nice piece of mince pie have I eaten at your mother's."

There were six Hawley boys who became lawyers—all honest lawyers, which I suppose would seem almost a contradiction in terms to our puritan sires. They were Henry T. Grout, Hezekiah Ryland Warriner, Charles Dodge, Samuel T. Field, P. L. Page and J. S. Page. The four last were near of an age, and attended the district school together in Hawley.

Well, I never knew a native of Hawley who went out from there into the world, to disgrace his native town. I am rejoiced that its history is to be written, and shall be glad if I have given any items that will be of use. Please let me know when it is published, and where copies can be obtained.

Very truly yours,
P. L. PAGE.

Ann Arbor, Mich., Dec. 1, 1886.

Sketches and Incidents.

The Rev. Jonathan Grout was an inveterate tobacco smoker. He lived about a hundred rods from the meeting house, and used to go home to dinner, between the two long Sunday services. On one occasion, when returning for the afternoon service, the fire from his pipe got into the fence by the roadside. The alarm was given in the midst of the sermon, when the services stopped, the congregation rushed out and extinguished the fire, returning for the minister to take up part fifthly of his sermon.

To show how long continued habit becomes second nature, and to show the force of absent-mindedness, it is related of him that he was once searching the house, having his pipe in his mouth, and addressed his wife thus:— "Mrs. Grout, can you tell me where I laid my pipe?"

Mr. Grout was cotemporary with Rev. Moses Hallock of Plainfield, and as might be inferred, they had many ministerial interviews. Mr. Hallock is described as being a tall, spare man, with sharp, angular features, and a very measured, methodical manner of speech. On one occasion when they were together, Mr. Grout was smoking an unusually short pipe, when Mr. Grout remarked that he should think he would burn his nose, whereupon Mr. Grout replied, "I should if my nose was as long as yours."

A family in Mr. Grout's parish kept geese, and the old gander had a habit of pecking on the door. One day Mr. Grout came to make a pastoral call, and knocking at the door, the good housewife, being busy about her work, and mistaking the familiar rapping, remarked, "Peck away, old gander, you can't come in."

David Scott of Whately, known as "Master Scott," was a man of great originality, a farmer, and carpenter, also a great hunter. (See page 42.) His son, Phineas, was the pioneer Scott in Hawley, and removed from Whately in 1782. He had previously been there and made a little clearing and built a log house, covering the roof with bark. When they moved he had a yoke of steers two years old, and a cow, and with his family, household furniture and farming tools on a sled, they went the first day to the west part of Conway, where they found it so blocked with snow that they were obliged to stop. The settlers turned out with teams and shovels and went through, and, hitching on their teams, pulled them through to their house, when lo! they found the roof had been so loaded with snow that it had broken in. Such was the introduction of one family to their newly-founded home. Mr. Scott was a farmer, an energetic, go-ahead man. Had done yeoman's service in the Revolutionary army. A man of integrity, and considerable prominence in his adopted town. Two of his children were born in Whately, and the others in Hawley.

In the old sixth school district is a lot of land which has always been known as the "Hitchcock lot," which was never transferred by deed. Before the settlement of the town, the territory was surveyed, the surveyors taking land in payment for their services. Among the party was a Mr. Hitchcock, whose son was subsequently one of the original settlers. This lot was taken by Mr. Hitchcock, though he never occupied it himself—it being probable that he never saw it after becoming its owner—and its ownership has passed by inheritance through successive generations to its present owner, Joseph A. Hitchcock, who was born there, now being the head of the only family bearing the name in town. It has formerly been occupied as a homestead, but now the buildings are removed, and it is occupied as an "out lot," a part of it being pasture.

In the near vicinity of the Hitchcock lot, on the farm formerly occupied by Ansel Hemenway, is the celebrated "Moody spring." The water from this spring is very medicinal, very soft and smooth in quality, preserving its natural qualities for any length of time, when kept in bottles or barrels, without becoming sour or rancid. It also has the power of removing any musty or inoffensive qualities from an old barrel or jug, and is a great curative for cutaneous diseases, leaving the skin in a healthy, normal condition. Quantities of the water have been carried considerable distances for use. There no doubt that if its approaches were more feasible, and some enterprising citizen would work up a boom by erecting fashionable buildings and attractive surroundings, it might rank favorably with watering places and summer resorts. But with its present surroundings, it must, as in the past, remain in comparative obscurity, and contribute very little for the "healing of the nations."

Rowland Sears bought land of parties in Springfield, on which he settled, being on the north line of the town, where his son Benjamin, and grandson of the same name, both lived and died, now owned and occupied by Lewis W. Temple. He did not make payment in full at the time of purchase, and afterward sent his neighbor, Ebenezer Hall, to make the settlement, and final payment, going on horseback. After completing the business, which was at a business office, Mr. Hall took his departure for home, and cogitating the matter in his mind, he discovered that an error had been made. Retracing his journey, he went to the office and told them he had returned to rectify a mistake. He was bluntly informed that they never made or rectified mistakes there. "Very well," said Mr. Hall, "I think I can stand it if you can; the mistake was in your favor."

Benjamin Sprague who lived in the east part of the town in its early history had a habit of making unwarrantable statements when relating or describing anything, and there is a tradition that when some one questioned a statement he had made, he said he hoped his hair would turn white, if it was not true, and the next morning it was actually white.

Clesson Smith lived a little west of the Square, and was known as an inveterate story teller. Some of the older people now living remember the yarns he used to tell, in which himself was usually the hero of the occasion. Whether he thought people would believe his recitals, or or whether he wanted to become notorious, or what his real object was, is still an open question. Once his daughter was taken with a fit in the night, and cramped so that her head and feet came together. He went for his horse in the pasture, some distance away, while a violent thunder shower was raging, repelled a flash of lightning with his fist, passed on and found his horse, went four miles for a doctor, and got him to the house in fifteen minutes after starting for the horse.

Once he was loading hay in the field, when a shower arose. He made such speed in driving to the barn that he escaped the rain; but his dog, not being able to keep up, was obliged to swim to the barn, through the accumulating waters.

Another of his exploits was to draw 200 loads of manure from the barn to the field in a day, with an ox team.

Warriner King, when a schoolboy, soon after the year 1800, attended school near the present site of Hallockville—being the same school where his cousin, Jonas King, was a scholar—more than a mile from his home, making his own track through the snow a part of the way. During one winter term he built the fire at the schoolhouse, which was in a large, open fire-place, his only remuneration being the ashes, which he collected and sold, and with the proceeds purchased a copy of "The American

Preceptor," the reading book in vogue in those days. Its title page bears the date, "Boston, 1801." About 1850, he gave it to the author of this work, and narrated the incidents above stated. It is highly valued as a relic, with its ancient and sombre appearance.

Jonas King was once a student at Halifax, Vt., at a school which was in some degree a self-supporting institution. It was a custom for the students to chop the wood they used, but Jonas was so engrossed in his studies that he preferred them to manual labor, so much so that he was "dubbed" as being lazy. But dire necessity compelled him to perform the task, and a brother student penned the following satire, and clandestinely placed it upon his door:—

"*Mirabile dictu*, Marcy on us,
Lament the fate of poor King Jonas;
Who from his high exalted station,
Is doomed to wield the axe for recreation."

Oliver Taylor received encouragement in various ways, in early life, to pursue his studies. The family was poor, and could not give him the advantages he desired, even in his youth. One winter several families in the east part of the town agreed to take turns in boarding him, while attending school there. In his early years he is described as not being very prepossessing, but made an education his only purpose and object. One evening when he was at Capt. John King's, some one proposed that he try his hand at poetry, when he produced these lines:—

"Cold and stormy is the weather,
Hard and wretched is my heart;"

They were written on his slate, and were the extent of his effusion. After he had retired for the night, Capt. King jokingly and wickedly added:—

"You simple, shatter-headed fellow,
From my house you may depart."

It may be added that the sentiment and decision expressed by those lines were both revoked, and Oliver was allowed to continue his studies, with what success is attested by the reputation he attained in after life.

When Rufus Sears came to Hawley he was a boy of 11 years. Coming from the "Cape," his early childhood had been identified with people of a seafaring life, and he had been accustomed to looking out upon the broad expanse of salt water. His minority, after coming to Hawley, was passed with Dea. Joseph Bangs, and after attaining his majority, he returned to the Cape, in the fall of the year, intending to remain and settle there. But during the winter, the scenes of ocean experiences did not look as flattering as he had anticipated, and in the spring he returned to Hawley, where he remained through his long life.

When he left Dennis the farmers were planting; arriving at the hills east of the Connecticut river and looking westward, the landscape was white, and arriving at Hawley, the people were still under the embargo of the winter's snow.

At a town meeting held May 6, 1799, it was voted to accept a road from Camp rock west to Savoy line. This rock is a little east of the house of Chester F. Hunt, and a little north of the site of the Theophilus Crosby house. It stands in a smooth field, and its highest point is about fifteen feet high, sloping each way from its apex to the ground, having a length of perhaps 50 feet, running north and south. Its eastern face is smooth and nearly perpendicular the entire length, while the west side is a sharp incline from top to bottom, making it something the shape of a quarter of an egg, cut lengthwise.

It is said that when Thomas King came to Hawley, in the spring of 1772, with his family, this rock was made a camping place over night, hence the origin of the name, "Camp rock." By its peculiar shape, it made a natural protection from the west wind, and a stream near by furnished water. Whether this place was appropriated as a camping-place for only one night, or while they prospected for a location, tradition saith not. The spot where Mr. King located and built was about a mile and a half west of this rock.

Somewhere about the year 1850, a woodchuck brought some bones out of its hole, in the West Hawley cemetery. They remained there upon the ground several weeks, attracting many visitors, and causing much speculation. It was not known to whose remains they belonged, until an examination was made, when a plate was found, showing it was the body of Joseph Howard, who had been buried many years. The woodchuck had entered at one end of the coffin and traversed its entire length, making the abode of the dead its home.

Hawley, like other towns, had a military company in the primitive times of the old State militia. In those old days ardent spirits were deemed a necessity, and were very freely brought into requisition on all occasions of that kind. Elias Goodspeed was captain of the company, and for some reason became unpopular with his men. On one occasion when they met for drill, he called them into line, and when the order "Forward March" was given, they started, but could not hear the command "Halt," and marched up plump against a building. Similar maneuvers were repeated, and the men were found to be incorrigible, when another captain was chosen, but the spirit of rebellion had detracted so much from the true military spirit, and the law requiring regular military drill having previously been taken off, the company disbanded in 1834, although some of the Hawley militia afterwards joined companies in adjoining towns.

On Monday evening, March 7, 1887, a great reception was held in Pittsfield, in honor of Hon. Henry L. Dawes, and his re-election to the U. S. Senate. Among the letters read was one from P. L. Page, of Ann Arbor, Mich., tendering congratulations and contributing this sentiment:—

<blockquote>
Massachusetts, and the equal rights of man; Fought for on her soil, in the first battle of the Revolution, at Lexington, and Concord.

Maintained by the first blood shed in the war for the preservation of the Union by her sons, in the streets of Baltimore.

Contended for by her distinguished legislators, John Quincy Adams and Charles Sumner, in our National Congress, in behalf of the African; and now by the senior senator of Massachusetts in behalf of the Indian. May his efforts be crowned with complete success.
</blockquote>

Roswell Longley was a great scholar, fitted for college, but his health failed and he was obliged to give up his studies, and died at the age of 33. The following was written by him as an Acrostic:—

<blockquote>
Hung up 'neath rocks and Nature's battlements she stands,

And towards high Heaven she lifts her giant, outstretched hands;

Waked by the eagle's cry, rocked by the stormy blast,

Long may she stand, to tell of ages past.

Earth has no nobler clime, no race of men more brave,

Youth, Age, and Beauty there, but not one cringing slave.
</blockquote>

Asa Vining, with his family, came from Weymouth to Hawley in 1806, arriving at the Connecticut river, at a point opposite Northampton, June 6, the day of the execution of Daley and Halligan. The rush was so great in consequence of the hanging that they could not cross the ferry as they desired, and Mr. Vining made arrangements with the ferry company to do some work in payment of their passage, and thus secured a transit across the river.

On the farm of Atherton Hunt are some objects which deserve mention. Near the buildings are three chestnut trees which Mr. Hunt set out with his own hands, more than 70 years ago. This is mentioned from the fact that the chestnut is not a native on these hills.

"Aunt Charity's chair" is an old landmark, being a rock by an old discontinued roadside, in which is a depression, making, by its shape and height from the ground, a natural seat.

Just east of Mr. Hunt's buildings there runs a long, narrow strip of swamp, which has been reclaimed, making good meadow land. There is a tradition that when one of the settlers came into town, his wagon became mired, and was overturned while crossing that swamp, and some table knives were lost. Mr. Hunt states that he has always had an eye open when working there, but never discovered any of the lost knives.

Reminiscences of a Former Resident.

WRITTEN BY P. F. COOLEY OF PITTSFIELD.

My earliest recollections of the old town where I first saw the light are very pleasant, and I love, in imagination, to again look out from the old east chamber over the hills and valleys, where in the distance can be seen the proud Mt. Wachusett, lifting its head above all its surroundings. Turning to the northeast, plainly outlined is the broad-based, yet equally towering Mt. Monadnock, while facing eastward, is the valley of the Connecticut river, which is often curtained by dense fogs, which sometimes in early mornings extended over and covered its entire length.

Our neighboring farmers used to say that fog on the river for three continuous mornings betokened rain. In fact, the broad expanse over which we could look became a sort of barometer, guiding the agriculturist in his daily calculations about what work to do, and what to postpone until the weather predictions should be favorable. In fact, all the observing men of that time were a self constituted signal service corps, and in justice I must say they were as reliable as some of the modern ones.

In those days of sparse settlers, and in the scarcity of reading matter, such as books and daily papers, it was very customary, as they met, to compare their prophetic skill, pertaining not only to rain, but also to what might be expected in the coming winter. If the corn husks were thick and heavy it was concluded that a hard winter was to come. If the muskrats were slow in making their holes in early autumn a long and pleasant fall was to be enjoyed. If the autumn winds howled with a peculiar noise around the farm buildings, it would be a time when they would find themselves short for hay in the spring. If, after a shower, the fog climbed up the sides of the hills, it would be fair on the next day, but if it settled into the valleys it would be a "catching" time for harvesting till after the next good shower had come and gone. In short, there was a sign for almost everything, and each event had a sign preceding it. When the time for "hog-killing" came, it must be done in the full of the moon, and the hog must receive the death stroke while the tide was coming in, or the pork would shrink in the pot. When the cat washed her face, the direction of her paw showed which way the wind would blow the next day. During a rain if a rooster crowed on the fence it would soon be fair, but if he crowed standing on the ground, the rain would continue until another day.

I can recall numerous signs like specimens given, which were by universal consent considered as infallible by the old settlers; some of which I learned from tradition, and others I heard from the lips of the descendants of that old puritan stock which settled in the town when it was an unbroken forest, and had to be subdued by the slow, hard work of the pioneer.

The east part of the town was settled by people coming from the eastern part of the state, from all the way as far as Cape Cod. My grandfather, Noah Cooley, came on horseback from Palmer in Hampden county, guided by blazed trees to indicate his road, and built a house (shanty it was termed) near the dividing line of Hawley and Buckland, in the primeval forest. The country was then filled with game, such as would be rare sport for the huntsmen of to day, consisting of black bears, raccoons, wolves, lynx and foxes, the latter of which were very plenty and quite tame. After felling the trees and making a clearing sufficient to raise a few potatoes and some corn, he built a barn near by for his horse and cow, for which he had to return to Palmer on foot, and drive back, making a journey of about 120 miles, both ways. He also combined pleasure with business, and at the same time paid his future wife a visit, which visits he annually kept up for seven years, at the expiration of which time, by diligent and hard work he had so far made a home in the wilderness that he had erected a more commodious house, and cleared more land and put it under cultivation, so that on the eighth year Esther Hyde accompanied him as his wife to the home he had thus prepared, he on horseback, she riding behind on a pillion. Their outfit of housekeeping goods, which she had been all those eight years in preparing, was hauled by a yoke of oxen attached to a two wheeled cart, the only wheeled vehicle then in common use. This manner of settlement by my grandfather is a sample of what was in almost every case the experience of the early settlers of the town. As a sequence, the pioneers grew up a hardy, self-reliant people, both men and women. They were brave and daring, and a community strongly religious and conscientious was the outcome of those descendants of the Puritan, obeying the command to be "fervent in spirit," and their necessities required them to be "diligent in business."

It will be my purpose in these pages to reproduce by a pen picture as I remember in part, and in part as has been described to me, the peculiarities and characteristics of some individuals who were prominent in town in its early days, beginning at the eastern part, which was earliest settled, and where my Hawley life was for the most part spent.

DEA. ISAAC TOBEY.

One of the early settlers in the extreme northeast part was Dea. Isaac Tobey, a native of Taunton, Mass. I am unable to tell at what age he came to town, but he must have been somewhat advanced in years, as he had previously been a soldier in the Revolution. It is said of him that when young he was a natural athlete, and could stand behind any man of common stature and vault completely over his head.

My earliest recollection of him as a boy was as an old man of about 75 or 80 years of age, straight as an arrow, not tall, of slight build, full of energy, and fully believing the generation had much deteriorated, both mentally and in industry. His son John, with whom he lived, was a perfect contrast to the father, remarkably large and stout, weighing nearly or quite two hundred and fifty pounds. He had a good education, and his lymphatic build compelled him to a literary and sedentary occupation, in fact, the deacon considered him lazy. I well recollect on one occasion hearing the old pensioner remark, "John don't like to work as well as I did," adding, after a pause, "Don't know as I say right; he don't like the profits of it as well." At the age of eighty five or more, the old deacon would with cane in hand every day visit the farm work as carried on by his grandsons, and suggest how the work should be done, which advice was not always acceptable to the boys, who were not particularly pleased with his frequent visits, yet his demeanor could but inspire them with respect for the old gentleman, as they usually called him. On one occasion when the boys were piling logs on a piece of land they were clearing, the old deacon came out as usual, and seated himself on a log near the pile they were making, when the log rolled over, throwing him on his back, between that and the pile. The boys were quite alarmed, fearing he was badly hurt, for he did not speak, and taking hold of him carefully, they began slowly and gently to lift him out. All at once, the old man spoke out in strong, commanding tones, "Lift, boys, Lift! you don't lift worth a copper." As might be expected, the boys speedily placed him on his feet.

At another time when mowing in the hayfield, one of the boys came across a bumblebees' nest, directly in his swath. The bees came out and sharply attacked the lad, who retreated, fighting them with his hat. The old deacon was near and saw the affair, and rushing up to the lad, exclaimed, "What, afraid of a few little bumble bees? Let me take your scythe." Taking the unfinished swath, he commenced mowing, but the bees were getting more troublesome and quite mad at being thus disturbed. Finally the old man laid down the scythe and stamped down the nest with his feet, then turning to the boy, he said, "Josh, you ain't got much pluck." He then started for the house, but the boys could see that he often rubbed his face, legs and arms, quite sharply, but his "pluck" was too good to own that the bees had stung him at all.

He was an honorable man in all his transactions, and well fitted by his life to adorn the position he held so long in the church as one of the deacons. He dated his first religious impressions in youth, from while walking with a comrade of his own age. A lightning bolt struck down his companion and killed him by his side, and from that time he made up his mind that he would live a christian life. His health was always good, and he wore out, dying at the age of over ninety.

Like every early New England town, Hawley had its village "Squire" to whom all questions of law and matters of dispute were referred, and

EDMUND LONGLEY,

one of the early settlers, living near the then populated center, occupied that honorable position. My first knowledge of him was when he was well advanced in life. He was then hale, and in my boyish eyes, a perfect pattern of all that was noble and great. He and his brother Joseph came from Groton, Mass. His house was larger and more imposing than most of his neighbors, and he was possessed of more worldly goods than most of his townsmen. The Longleys by nature were of a strong, sterling character, of the sort born to command. In fact, three of his sons were military commanders in days when the arms-bearing men were all required to do military duty. One was a Brigadier general, another a Colonel, and a third a Captain in the Massachusetts militia of that day. As the pages of this history show, Esquire Longley and his descendants occupied many and varied places of trust in the affairs of the town. So honorable a position was accorded to many of that name, that a few years ago a quaint old divine in the town of Dalton remarked to me, "Your Hawley folks always thought the Longleys made the town." At all events, the Longleys had much to do in shaping the annual town meetings and giving general direction to all affairs of the town. To be able to do so, shows that the material from which such stock descended is of no ordinary type. Such men, to rule others, must be of the kind who can rule themselves. As an illustration, when Squire Longley was well advanced in years he made up his mind that tobacco, which he had constantly used from boyhood, was doing him no good, and as soon as he thus decided, he took out his pipe and a partly used paper of tobacco and laid them on the mantle shelf over the open fireplace, in plain sight, and wrote on the tobacco package, "Tobacco, I have done with you," and there it remained untouched until he was gathered to his fathers, at a ripe old age.

In the adjoining town of Buckland was a family of Taylors who occupied the same position in that town that was accorded to the Longleys in Hawley, in fact, Squire Taylor of Buckland and Squire Longley of Hawley were considered the two magnates of that region.

As might be expected, Squire Longley's eldest son, Thomas, (afterward Gen. Longley,) sought for a wife the eldest daughter of Squire Taylor, Martha, or "Patty" as the name was then called. After the arrangements between the young people had been completed, it became necessary, by a custom of the times, for Thomas to procure of his parents their consent to the union. For that purpose he called them into the parlor, and when they were solemnly seated, Thomas with all due formality made known the object of the interview, viz, their approval of his marriage with Patty Taylor. The Squire, from the dignity of his large arm chair, responded, "Yes, my son Thomas, I am happy to give my full and free consent, and am glad, as well as proud, to know that my son is to be allied to the family of my old friend, Squire Taylor of Buckland, and shall be pleased to own Patty as a daughter." The Squire's wife had a full and lively sense of humor, and saw a fine chance for a joke, even if it was at the expense of her son, also anticipated subsequent events somewhat. Leaning over a little on her side, and lightly tapping the floor with one foot, she said, "Tommy, I strongly suspect the next generation of Hawley children will make their own baskets."

Neither the Longleys or the Taylors were in complexion disposed to the blonde type, but on the contrary bordered on the brunette, and especially did the Taylors assume the type of the dark brunette, with hair of the same color, and straight, resembling that of the Indian.

For years there was hardly a school district in town but that had a representative of the Longley family, but now only one family of the name lives in town, that of Lewis Longley. Such are the changes effected in a few short years.   Squire Edmund, Master Joe, Uncle Ziba, Gen. Thomas, Capt. Edmund, Col. Joshua, Luther, Calvin S., Sullivan Otis, Freeman, Thomas, Joseph G., Worcester, Augustus, Roswell, Joshua and Oliver, faces and names familiar to my boyhood, have passed over, and others are removed, to Dakota, Illinois, Wisconsin, Washington, and in fact almost all over the Union are the descendants of that old Hawley name, scattered and widely separated.   Is it too much to hope that they and we all, in the future of God's good providence, will again be united, and again greet, and know each other as in days when we inhabited the eastern slope of the Green Mountains?

In the primitive days of all New England towns, the minister appeared as the most prominent personage. Being usually a man of a college education, to him was deputed the adjudication of questions where learning was required in rendering a decision. Often his talents were called in where it was necessary to assume judicial as well as ecclesiastical functions. The proper pronunciation of words, the geographical location of any new or unknown place, or any abstruse mathematical calculus, all were referred to the parson, and his decision was final, no appeal therefrom, while in all things having reference to biblical law, he was as a matter of course the sole judge, and even the place and condition one would occupy after death, he was supposed to have cognizance of. Woe be to the luckless, independent free thinker who dared to interpret scripture differently from this high authority.

On his approach childish glee and sports were hushed, and the juvenile heart beat fast and quick when in the august presence of the minister. When met upon the street each boy must remove his hat and make his best bow, each girl, with blushing face and downcast eyes, must drop her best curtsy. It is not for a moment to be supposed that Hawley was behind any New England town in all that pertained to ministerial etiquette. My earliest recollections of

PARSON GROUT

was fully up to the above general requirements. He was a large, robust, rotund personage, to my eyes the perfect embodiment of all that goes to make a man and a hero. Even to day I can in fancy hear his round, sonorous voice, as from the immensely high pulpit he read the hymns and invoked God's blessing or expounded the scriptures to his flock, which in those days included the whole town's people. Mr. Grout was the first settled minister in Hawley, and commenced preaching when it was called No. 7, before its incorporation as a town. Of Mr. Grout's ability as a preacher, in consequence of my youth I was not competent to judge, but do know that as a good man and a faithful preacher, to his death he was held in high esteem, not only by his own flock but also by those of other and adjoining towns. In deportment he was uniformly cheerful, but never hilarious. According to the custom of those days, when making parochial calls he readily partook with his host of the universal flip or egg nog, but never were his potations so deep as to make any showing either in his face, carriage or speech. He spent his whole ministerial life in the town, and under his teaching there grew up a healthy, strongly religous community, who to day, wherever found, are God-fearing, Sabbath-loving men and women. As a result of the teachings of this faithful servant of the Most High, there has emanated from the town a large corps of ministers, now scattered throughout the country, who in their stalwart christianity bear the imprint of their first teacher. Mr. Grout died at a ripe old age, and on his tombstone is chiselled in many lines the regards of his former parishioners, in words of no ambiguous import.

THE OLD MEETING HOUSE.

To an absent son or daughter of Hawley, probably no one thing in connection with the old town is more deeply graven on the memory than the old house of worship, where from early years to manhood we listened Sabbath after Sabbath to the instructions that came from that old high pulpit, or the voices from the well filled "singers' seats," loftily perched at the opposite end from the minister. How freshly, even to day, do I recall the ideas of my young boyhood, as riding in the family wagon, on a Sunday morning, when the view of that old church first broke on my vision. To me it was a symbol of all that was large, grand, lofty and holy. Nearly square in form, its two stories were well adorned with large windows, and a huge, two storied porch was equally well lighted with windows a trifle smaller, one large entering door facing the east, which was reached by several stairs. On either side of of this double storied porch were smaller doors where those approaching from the north and south sides respectively, could enter. My earliest vision of the sacred old building was when it was a dingy yellow, but in later years when its weather-beaten clapboards showed signs of exposure to the elements it was painted white, which color it bore until its final demolition for a more modern structure in a new location near the old "red store," two miles south. Beside the door, on the right, was a glass-faced box for posting notices of all kinds pertaining to religious and secular business. Also an important mission this box had to fill was the publishing on three consecutive Sundays, a notice, bearing the official signature of the Town Clerk, of any parties who proposed soon to marry. From this latter use this box was in common parlance dubbed the "publishing box." Regularly on each Sabbath morning this box was scanned by the young of both sexes, and often by the older people, to see what two persons proposed soon to exchange single for married life. When such notices appeared, it was a theme, that in the hour of intermission occupied no small part of the conversation. At times, these marriage notices would be a surprise, but oftener it was the culmination of an anticipated event, which caused much solicitude by scrutinizing neighbors and friends.

Having thus surveyed its outward appearance, now go with me inside and let us together see if we can not only reproduce its interior in general, but also place in old niches objects and faces once so familiar to us. As we enter the lower porch we find, leading to the gallery, two flights of stairs, one on either hand, corresponding to the side doors for entrance, mounting either of which, we find quite an upper room or vestibule for waiting, until the time for services to begin. Right in front, is another flight of stairs extending the whole width of this upper porch which led to the final entrance of the gallery. The gallery extended around three sides of the main audience room, with seats fitted for singers in front, and along the sides as well, flanked in the rear by square pews with plain seats which turned back on iron hinges. From these distant and lofty boxes the worshipper had to look down not a little to see the minister, and from the seats near the wall he could not, even by hard craning of the neck, be visible. I imagine there are now living gray haired men and women who well remember the corner pews where they often congregated out of sight of minister and parents, and during those long sermons said and did things not in keeping with the puritan Sabbath or the sanctity of the place. Below, you will recollect the roomy broad aisle, standing in which, you have seen candidates for admission to the rites of the church, and parents holding their infants for baptism. In this broad aisle, too, you have seen young couples, as they presented themselves to take the vows that made them twain one flesh. The last occasion of the kind I witnessed there was when the now dead, but once celebrated Dr. Stephen R. Riggs proudly led the granddaughter of Esq. Longley up this wide avenue, and after the ceremony was performed he alone stood in the same spot, then and there was consecrated as the first missionary to the Dakota Indians, of the tribe called Sioux. On that occasion, which was on a week day, the old church was crowded to its fullest capacity. My impressions on that occasion were as that of a very solemn event. Dr. Riggs and wife directly went to their chosen field, and spent their young, as well as their mature lives, in vigorous efforts to elevate that warlike tribe, the results of which, he graphically portrays in his book, "Mary and I."

But let us go back to the old church and see if we cannot see familiar faces. It is a Sabbath morning; way up in that lofty pulpit is the venerable Jonathan Grout, his head mantled by a snowy crown, and his full voice ringing out as he conducts the exercises. Directly underneath are seated the two equally venerable looking deacons, on the right of the pulpit is the minister's family pew, and on the left is the pew occupied jointly by the families of Edward Porter and Stephen Damon. Squarely in front, on the right of the broad aisle, is the pew of "Master Joe Longley," next in the rear is the Sabbath home of Squire Edmund Longley, directly opposite is the town doctor Forbes and family, and in front of these are two long wooden seats fronted by a high partition, which are for the deaf. If the gospel sound cannot penetrate their ears it can fall on their heads with heavy effect, so far below the minister do they sit.

When the meeting house was built, no provision was made for warming it, no chimney, or place left for one. Being rather cheaply covered, with only clapboards and plastering to keep out the winter's cold, the thermometer would register about the same inside as out.

There is a time when patience ceases to be a virtue, and at length the women became tired of going to the neighbors' houses to fill their footstoves, and a demand came to procure stoves and warm the house. This met with a fierce opposition, and a portion of the congregation strongly maintained that those who could not sit in the cold, lacked religious fervor in their hearts. After a long discussion, and not a little hot contention, it was decided to get two stoves, and to insure full results, two long lines of pipe were extended from the stoves near the deaf men's seat entirely across the room, giving them an exit at a window each side of the main entrance, expecting the room would thus be made comfortable.

Vain delusion! On the cold mornings so often prevailing on that windy mountain top, it was impossible, even then, to keep comfortable at the farther end of the room, even when wrapped in the traditional surtout.

It was, however, quite noticeable that those who had at the first so hotly opposed the introduction of stoves were the first to appropriate them, and lingered longest near their genial warmth. The building was so poorly covered that it was impossible to equally warm it. Capt. King used to say that one might as well warm an acre out of doors.

But if the building was cheaply covered, it was strongly built. Heavy and ponderous timbers were used in the framework, and a comical man once remarked that the timbers were so huge that it took a barrel of rum to raise it, a remark that seemed to me quite pithy, when in process of demolition I saw those huge, hard wood timbers uncovered.

Farewell, old meeting house! Around thee cluster many tender and ennobling memories. Within thy doors have many entered who there found comfort in hours of trial, consolation in times of distress. Within thy sacred walls have many an one been instructed, and led to a higher and nobler life. Within thy courts has many a new born soul found peace, and sang a new song.

A history of Hawley, and particularly of its first meeting house, would hardly be complete without some notice of its surroundings. To one long absent from the town of his birth, a remembrance of the old church as it was, necessarily takes in objects in its near vicinity. Directly north of the church, and on a little lower ground, was

THE OLD SANFORD PLACE,

a large, pretentious building of two stories, and a long ell running out towards the west. It had never been adorned with paint, but the elaborate carvings and exterior adornments gave evidence that it had been a place in which its owner felt not a little pride, in fact, William Sanford was at a time looked upon as the millionaire of Hawley. At one time he kept a "tavern" in the upright part, and in the ell was a general country store. Tradition says that at that store was sold more wet than dry goods. When it was considered reputable to buy and sell ardent spirits, Sanford's was thought the best place to buy New England rum, and selling it as he did, by the barrel, and down in lesser quantities till it reached the single drink, it did afford him a good revenue.

Mr. Sanford was a pushing, wide-awake Yankee, of stalwart build, blessed with a good constitution. He often took large and laborious contracts of work, such as road-building, etc., and it was said that he could hire help that would perform more work than others, for two reasons; one was, a man must put forth considerable effort to keep up with his employer, another was, the extra stimulus, so handy, gave them an unusual amount of push and vim. What mattered it if there was little or nothing due them at settlement? for they had had a good time drinking, instead of laying up their wages. Many are the tales I have heard from my elders of the sprees had at the old Sanford tavern, and of the variety of expedients devised by the landlord to make trade brisk at the bar, such as guessing on the weight of a block of wood, or even a stone by the roadside, the loser to treat the crowd. The knowing ones used to say that the landlord was never or seldom caught, for secretly he had weighed and measured all articles upon which he proposed a guess. While the better class of citizens deprecated such measures and censured the revelries at the tavern, it was noticeable that at times of festal gatherings in the ample hall of that house, it was well patronized, and numbers of the above mentioned critics were present.

As wealth increased, so did a desire for honors, and by virtue of a commission from the Governor, Mr. Sanford received the title, "Esq," as a prefix or adjunct, as the case might demand. Causes of some import were often tried before Squire Sanford, partly, because of his commodious hall, and also because it was so very convenient to find means to allay the thirst consequent upon contested lawsuits. With large sales at his bar on such occasions and the added legal fee, his increasing coffers constantly received accumulations, to make up the fortune he left at his death. But as is uniformly the case in our American society, the next generation scattered these accumulations much faster than the Squire had gathered them in.

It would have been a high honor to any town, that it was the birthplace of

JONAS KING, D. D.,

a missionary to Greece, and for years the U. S. Consul there. Springing from almost total obscurity, he occupied in after years, a position as one of the foremost men of the age. His early home, all natives of Hawley know, was removed from all opportunities to grow up a polished and refined boy, but the germs of a strong manhood was an inherent quality in his composition. Never did a youth upon emerging from a retired home, find himself more unsophisticated than did young King when he commenced teaching his first school in the old third district. But of all this he very well knew, and was not ashamed to confess it, and use all possible methods to improve. After a gathering of young people for an evening entertainment, he would ask a trusted friend if he had said anything that was wrong, awkward, or green, or if he had used correct language when addressing a lady, or if he had properly used his handkerchief or knife and fork. He would go out of a room and imagine the room a place of gathering, asking for instructions as to his deportment when entering. Ridicule only had the effect of making him try to so deport himself as not to again be its subject. Advice he sought from all alike, belles, matrons, and male companions, and was ready to accept it from any. A perfectly unpolished diamond in youth, which never lost anything in polishing and resetting.

Although many of that family name formerly lived in that locality, giving it the title King Corner, it is with pride that former residents refer to it as the town where Rev. Dr. King was born. He was a grandson of Thomas King the pioneer, and his son, Ezra, and his grandson, Warriner, passed their lives in the same neighborhood, also the father of Dr. King, on another road but little used in travel.

No native of the town can fail to remember

UNCLE EPHRAIM MARSH.

In boyish remembrance I again meet him, going with two crutches, a short, pendant stump taking the place of a long lost leg, as he went from place to place, disposing of wooden measures of his own manufacture, which contributed largely to his support. Neither shall I forget the half dread I felt when meeting him, for he would stop and press home upon the boy some searching question relative to his spiritual welfare. These questions were propounded alike to all he met, regardless of age, sex or condition. I have been informed that his early life was spent as a sailor, and that he was exceedingly rough and profane, but being brought under religious influence, his life became a perfect contrast to what it had been. "Where sin did abound, grace did more abundantly abound." Often has he asked me, "My boy, do you love the Lord, and pray to him?" a salutation common with him. He was a constant attendant at all Sabbath services, and equally constant at the prayer meetings. Totally uneducated and uncouth in speech, his remarks, although inspiring one, would, by their original and ungrammatical form, provoke a smile, sometimes quite audible, hardly decorous in a prayer meeting. As an example, I quote one verbatim, made in one of his public prayers;— "O Lord, come with thy holy spirit, and wake up these sleepy young lambs; yes, good Lord, and stir up the old sheep too. O Lord, you and I both know they need it." Yet he was a man universally loved and respected, for he had a kind disposition and a warm heart. His deep, heartfelt earnestness impressed all he met that he was a christian man. He fully met the description of the man who "lived and died happy, for he loved and served his God."

I have in mind one who was a sharp contrast to Mr. Marsh,

UNCLE HOLLISTER BAKER,

a man upright in all his transactions, in full possession of all his faculties, and exerted them to their utmost to the accumulation of wealth. Everything with him must bow to that one supreme object; education, popularity or religion he cared nothing for. Money was his idol, and before that shrine he was a devout worshipper. On one occasion his pastor, urging upon him the necessity of taking some thought for a future life, and not be engrossed with worldly matters to its neglect, enforced his subject with the remark, "Bro. Baker, you know that money takes to itself wings and flies away." "Know it, know it, better put it into land." was uncle Hollister's reply.

Near his early home lived Ebenezer Crowell, whose daughter he sought for a wife, and having obtained the girl's consent, it was necessary to get the consent of her parents. He deputed his father for that duty who thus approached it:— "Neighbor Crowell, my son Hollister woold be glad to have your dafter Becky, I'm jealous; he woold if he coold I'm jealous." What the answer was I never learned, but must have been in the affirmative, as they were duly married, and raised a large family.

In the same neighborhood lived Dea. ZENAS BANGS, a farmer who always performed his work in a slovenly manner. It used to be said of him that he would tire out a dog following him when mending brush fence. He had a neighbor who swept out his hog pen every day, including Sundays. Once on his way to church it occurred to him that he had neglected the usual sweeping, and going back to perform that duty, they were late to church, a sin almost inexcusable those days. But his good wife, Aunt Lizzie, explained the situation to the critics, by informing them that she had cut his hair that morning, which made him forget all about the pig-pen.

West Hill, Bozrah, Forge Hollow, the Square, King Corner, Hallockville, South Hawley, Red Store, Hunt district, Dodge neighborhood, Parker Hill.— Absent sons and daughters of old Hawley! do not these names of familiar locations call up interesting and tender memories?

Lads and girls then, now gray-haired and gone, cannot let slip from the pages of memory the many singing schools in which they met and practiced the musical scale as taught by Col. Barr, Mr. Ford, and by their fellow townsman, Taylor Grout, where they not only practiced and sang the songs of Zion, but where were often exchanged sly glances, and equally sly pressure of hands on the road home, little courtesies which in many cases culminated in the union of two hearts and a happy home, perhaps in the far west, or perhaps a settlement on the homestead to solace the declining years of loved and loving parents.

And those old time district spelling schools; how fresh and vividly do they return, with other old time pleasures, as memory reverts to the old town and its inhabitants, and wherever we roam, we fully endorse the sentiment, as we sing, "Be it ever so humble, there's no place like home."

APPENDIX.

The following items have been gleaned from various sources, since the compilation of the preceding chapters—

Much has already been said in this volume of Rev. Dr. King, but a tract published by the American Tract Society, entitled "The only Son" has just come to hand, from which we clip the following:—

In 1819 Mr. King was elected professor in Amherst College, and proceeded to Paris to pursue the study of Arabic with the celebrated De Sacy. Soon after, the Rev. Levi Parsons, missionary to Palestine, died, and Mr. King was solicited to supply his place in the missionary field. He was oppressed with the weight of the proposition, and sought the advice of an American gentleman there, with whom he had become acquainted, who was at the head of a large commercial house. His friend said, "Go, and I will be a son to your aged parents in America."

It was found that $1500 were necessary as an outfit for him to go, and the merchant volunteered $300 of the amount, and gave him the names and address of four friends in the different European states, to whom he could apply for the remaining $1200. By the return of the mails, these gentlemen responded, enclosing $300 each, making the sum required, and Mr. King lost no time in preparing for his departure.

Previous to this Mr. King had established religious meetings in Paris, and a large concourse assembled in the church of the Oratoire to listen to his farewell address, and he was cheered at different points on his way to Jerusalem. His friend, the merchant, wrote to the solitary parents from time to time, enclosing some token of regard "from their affectionate son." The next year he returned to America, and in the spring of 1824, he procured a team at Northampton, and freighting it with groceries, went twenty five miles to their humble abode in Hawley. He appeared in disguise, ostensibly stopping to warm, recognizing in them the features of their son. Soon he directed his conversation in such a way as to let them know who he was, when a very affecting scene followed. Then the groceries were presented, refreshments served, and during the repast the father was asked if he felt any regret in parting with his only son as a missionary, which question, with the answer, is engraved on his tombstone in Hawley. This interview was the only one ever held between them, and to the aged parents it was almost as a visit from their son.

The spot where the missionary is buried, in Athens, is in a retired corner, shaded by cypress and pepper trees, enclosed by an iron railing, supported at the corners by stone pillars. Over it is erected a white marble sarcophagus monument, said to be the gift of an affectionate daughter, on which is the following inscription:—

SACRED TO THE MEMORY OF JONAS KING, D. D.

He was born at Hawley, Massachusetts. United States of America, July 29, 1792. He labored for four years as a missionary in Palestine, and for upwards of forty years as a missionary in Greece, and died in Athens, May 22, 1869, in the 77th year of his age.

"I have fought a good fight, I have finished my course, I have kept the faith. Henceforth there is laid up for me a crown of righteousness."

2 Tim. 4: 7, 8.

Seth Sears was born July 27, 1801, is the oldest native resident, lives on West Hill. He m. May 19, 1827, Anna Stockwell. Their children were Sarah Ann, b. Aug. 13, 1828, Henry, b. Sept. 13, 1830, resides in Dalton, Silas S., b. Feb. 9, 1833, resides in Dalton, Roswell and Royal, b. May 7, 1835, reside in Hawley, Bethiah H., m. H. S. Barton, and lives in Savoy.

Roswell Sears m. Mary E. Pierce, Jan. 2, 1861. Children, Annie, b. July 9, 1863. m. John T. Carrington, Seth W., b. June 21, 1874.

Royal Sears m. Roselma Sturtevant. Children, Ernest R., b. Aug. 4, 1868, Herman E., b. March 27, 1870, Cora A., b. Jan. 20, 1872, Wesley E., b. April 9, 1874.

Children of Lewis W. and Ella (Sears) Temple; Eddie S., b. April 30, 1873, Bessie E., b. Sept. 4, 1876, Lizzie E. and Lida E., b. Nov. 6, '8

Three of the daughters of Theophilus Crosby married clergymen, viz: Saphronia married Rev. James McKee, and lives in Cairo, Ga., Sarah married Rev. Mr. Hodge, and lives in Oregon, Phebe married Rev. Mr. Crawford, and lives in Solon, Ind. (Corrected from page 22.)

Judah and Cutler Crosby are in Dakota.

Rufus Baker is living in Warren, Mass, at the age of 85.

Tryphena, daughter of Calvin Cooley married Leonard E Curtis, and resides in Iowa City.

Rev. Oramel W. Cooley resides at Glenwood, Ill.

A Mr. Noyes, born in Putney, N. H., founder of the Oneida community, once had a spirited discussion with Rev. Tyler Thatcher.

Annual Town Meeting, March 7, 1887:— Moderator, Wm. O. Bassett; Clerk and Treasurer, Lucius Hunt; Selectmen and Assessors, Charles Crittenden, J. Wm. Doane, Amos D. Taylor; School Committee, for 3 years, Justin B. Warriner, for 2 years, J. Wm. Doane; Constable and Collector, Adna Q. Bissell. Appropriations: Schools, $900; Highways and bridges, $1500; Town expenses; $1200; Total, $3600.

Teachers in the public schools, Spring term, 1887:— Dist. No. 1, Inez White, No. 2, Geo. Gould, No. 3, Mary Wells, No. 6, Hattie Simpson, No 7, Ida L. Brackett, No. 8, Carrie L. Atkins.

INDEX TO FAMILY RECORDS.

Atkins, Giles, Freeman, Isaac, Francis W., William G.,	page	65	Eldridge, Levi,	60
			Easton, Joseph,	53
Ayres, Wells,		46	Edgerton, Joseph,	101
Baker, Timothy, Hollister, Horace, Harvey,		45	Edgerton, Ezekiel,	102
			Fuller, Jonathan, Jonathan Jr.,	46
Baker, Roswell, Rufus, Joel,		46	Farnsworth, William,	46
Breed, John,		61	Ford, Elias,	58
Blood, Abner, Asa,		57	Ford, Noah, Elijah,	62
Baxter, Edward,		57	Field, Theodore,	67
Butrick, Joseph,		57	Fobes, Dr. Daniel,	61
Bassett, William,		58	Grout, Rev. Jonathan, Samuel T.	53
Beals, Otis,		59	Griggs Chester F.,	56
Bartlett, Joel,		59	Goodspeed, Elias,	57
Barnard, Joseph,		62	Gould, Aaron,	65
Bangs, Zenas, Zenas Jr., Joseph,		48	Gould, Lemuel, Wilson, Daniel H., Gilbert A., Luther E.,	66
Burt, Daniel,		46		
Crowell, Ebenezer, Edward, Ebenezer,		61	Graham, Zerah,	69
			Hall, Ebenezer, Ebenezer Jr., Samuel,	47
Crosby, Theophilus,		62		
Crosby, Judah, Eben,		63	Hall, Rufus,	61
Crittenden, Simeon,		67	Hall, Seth,	69
Clark, Samuel A., Phineas,		52	Hitchcock, Samuel, Ethan, Arthur, Joseph A.,	48
Cooley, Noah, Calvin, Calvin E., Reuben,		56		
			Hitchcock, Erastus, Samuel Jr., Simeon, Eli,	60
Cooley, Asher,		57		
Carrier, Elias,		58	Holden, Levi, Levi Jr., Ira,	51
Carter, Millo T., Sanderson, Ashbel W.,		60	Howes, Joseph, Edmund, Henry,	52
			Hunt, Atherton, Russell, Lucius, Chester,	55
Davis, Ozias,		67		
Damon, Jonathan,		59	Hunt, John, Elisha,	56
Dodge, Silas, Hiram,		62	Howard, Joseph,	57
Doane, James, James Jr., J. William,		63	Harmon, Levi, Gains, Enos,	59
			Hadlock, John,	59
Damon, Bardin,		63	Hawkes, Alpheus, Levi, Ichabod, Zadock, Asher,	66
Dickinson, Samuel, Ebenezer,		68		
Dyer, Anson,		52	Joy, Noah,	60
Darby, Edward,		66	King, Ezra, John,	45

King, Thomas, Jonas, Amos, Jotham,	page 44	Rice, Champion B., Luther, Moses, Elias,	55
Longley, Edmund,	42	Scott, Phineas, Reuben,	
Longley, Thomas, Capt. Ed-Luther, Joshua, Calvin S., Oliver S., S. Newell, Elijah F.,	43	Luther, Edwin,	42
		Sears, Clark,	58
Longley, Joseph, Zimri, Loren, Jonas P., James Sullivan,	44	Sears, Rufus, Anthony, Frederick H., Alvan, Urbane, Roland, Alden, Sylvester,	50
Lascombe, John,	54	Stiles, Warham, Garner,	53
Look, Henry,	50	Smith, Obed,	56
Loomis, Asher,	63	Simons, Uzziel,	58
Lathrop, Zephaniah,	68	Sprague, Rufus,	60
Lathrop, Zephaniah Jr.,	69	Sprague, William,	62
Marsh, Elijah, Ephraim, Leonard,	49	Starks, John, Phineas,	64
		Shattuck, Oliver,	64
Mc Intyre, William,	54	Sanford, William, William Jr.,	63
Mantor, James, Francis	57	Smith, Clesson,	61
Mansfield, Erastus,	67	Strong, Harvey,	68
Newton, Nathaniel,	57	Taylor, Jeremiah,	58
Oakes, Calvin, William, John,	49	Taylor, A. Dennis,	65
Parker, Abraham, Abraham Jr., James Monroe, Nathaniel,	47	Taylor, John, John Jr.,	64
		Thayer, Ebenezer,	61
Parker, Asa, Zenas,	48	Tobey, John,	69
Parker, David, Abel,	69	Upton, Chester,	60
Patch, Oliver,	67	Vincent, John,	52
Patch, William,	68	Vincent, Nathan, Joshua,	53
Pixley, Stephen,	68	Vining, Asa, David,	63
Porter, Ebenezer,	68	Wood, Zebedee, Andrew, Fitch,	67
Page, Alvah,	68	Warriner, Hezekiah,	68
Rogers, Abisha,	46, 47	Wheeler, Samuel,	65
Russell, Elihu,	46	West, Nathan,	64
Russell, Samuel, Spencer,	57	White, Henry B.,	61
Rogers, Moses,	68	Worthington, Timothy,	49
Rice, Jonas, Sylvanus, Daniel,	54	Wells, Jonathan,	62

ERRATA.

Page 21, Rev. Isaac Oakes was born in Hawley, instead of Hadley.
Page 25, Peter L. Baker enlisted, 1862, died, in 1877, at Bernardston, Mass., instead of Vt.
Page 37, Adonijah Taylor is probably John Taylor.
Page 41, Aaron Baird should read Aaron Burt.
Page 68, Alvah Page should be Phineas Page.

www.ingramcontent.com/pod-product-compliance
Lightning Source LLC
Chambersburg PA
CBHW021937160426
43195CB00011B/1122